Leaves From Sherwood Forest, By January Searle...

George Searle Phillips

THE NEW
POPULAR LIBRARY,

IN FANCY BOARDS, SIXPENCE EACH.

The following Works are issuing :—

CHAPTERS IN THE LIFE OF A DUNDEE
FACTORY BOY. Written by Himself.

PEN AND INK SKETCHES OF EMINENT
ENGLISH LITERARY PERSONAGES.

THE SEA-SIDE AND THE FIRE-SIDE : by
Professor Longfellow.

VOICES OF THE NIGHT, and OTHER
POEMS, by do.

THE LIFE OF DR. FRANKLIN.

ESSAYS : by ditto.

TALES FROM THE PARSONAGE.

THE YOUNG SAILOR : by Mrs. Dana.

LOITERINGS IN AMERICA, by the author
of " Pen and Ink Sketches."

LUCY SANDFORD : a Story of the Heart.

THE ORGANIZATION OF LABOUR AND
ASSOCIATION : by Briancourt.

TALES : from the German of C. V. Schmid.

LONDON:
CHARLES GILPIN, 5, BISHOPSGATE STREET.
And Sold by all Booksellers.

LEAVES

FROM

SHERWOOD FOREST.

BY JANUARY SEARLE,

AUTHOR OF "LIFE AT HOME AND ABROAD," ETC.

LONDON:

CHARLES GILPIN, 5, BISHOPSGATE STREET.

DUBLIN:—J. B. GILPIN.

—

MDCCCL.

DEDICATION.

TO MY BELOVED FRIEND

THOMAS SPENSER, ESQ.,

OF BRANSBY,

IN THE BEAUTIFUL VALLEY OF THE TRENT:

I DEDICATE THIS VOLUME.

J. S.

PREFACE.

I HAVE written this book, because I love the people and the scenes described in it; and if the reader will visit Sherwood, he will find that even the enthusiasm manifested by Charles Rees Pemberton, in the "Sketch" contained in these pages, is not without poetical warrant, in the beauty and magnificence of that fine sylvan domain.   I only regret that the limits prescribed to me, have shut out Washington Irving, and my good and gifted friend William Howitt, from the Forest Symposium of which these pages are the celebration. Few guests could have added more grace to the board, and I know none who would have been more heartily welcome.

J. S.

June 8th, 1850.

LEAVES FROM SHERWOOD FOREST.

IN the month of June last year, I was on a visit to my friend, the Rector of B——, in the valley of the Trent. The day of my arrival was one of those warm, sunny days, when Nature seems to put on her holiday attire, and rejoice over the green earth, with flowers and music in her train.

I had come upon the Great Cliffe Road from Lincoln, and turning down the old lane, by the park wall, leading to the little hamlet of B——, soon arrived at my friend's gate. A broad gravel walk, running between beds of shrubs and flowers, led me by the church and the grave-yard, to the Rectory. The gable ends of the old-fashioned looking house were covered with the glossy leaves of the ivy, which spread over the leaning roofs, and gave to the whole build-ing a very picturesque appearance.

After I had renewed my acquaintance with the great Newfoundland dog, whose kennel was

B

fixed opposite to the stables and coach-house, at the back of the Rectory, I made my way to the garden in front, where I beheld the good Rector seated under a large beech tree, and listening with evident interest, to what I afterwards found was Alfred Tennyson's new poem of " *The Princess*," which a beautiful young girl was reading to him aloud. I hid myself for a few moments, amongst the dark pines, at the foot of the terrace-walk, and tried to catch the music of the maiden's voice ; but the rooks kept up such a perpetual cawing, that I soon found it was impossible. I resolved, therefore, to give them a surprise, and accordingly, set up a great shout, which brought the Rector to his feet in a moment ; and whilst he and the lady were looking round, and wondering from what quarter, and from what uproarious lungs, the shout came, I suddenly darted from my hiding place.

It was now the Rector's turn to shout ; and to do him justice, he did it with a *furor*, worthy of any one of Homer's heroes,—sending his cap up into the air, at the same time, and bounding over the lawn to meet me. Our hands were soon grappled together, as if in mortal conflict, and I can feel the blood tingling at my finger's ends, from the manliness of that grip, even now whilst I am writing. There was no mistake about that meeting. Heart spoke to heart, through hands and eyes ; although I don't remember that there were many words uttered between us.

I am inclined to think the young lady thought us both mad; for she stood anxiously watching us during this alarming scene, puzzled to know how it would end. She was soon satisfied, however, in this particular; for my good friend, the Rector, introduced me to her as an old cronie from the North, and in a short time we were all deep in a conversation upon the merits of "*The Princess.*" I am not going to record here the wise remarks and shrewd criticisms, which occurred during that conversation; but will at once present my friends to the reader as people worth knowing, and whose company he will be glad to keep, for the day or two which these pages will embrace and occupy.

And first of all, the Rector. For although it is customary to speak of ladies before gentlemen —and I like to honour the observance of it in most cases—yet friendship has deeper claims than those of courtesy; and seeing also, that the Rector is master of his own house, and that I am his guest, it seems to me a matter of refinement and propriety to speak of him first. Therefore, I will try and tell you what he is like.

Fortunately I need not describe him by any negative process;—(as a witty friend of mine in Halifax once did, who, speaking of a certain editor, began his description of him by saying,

" he is *not* a decent fellow "—) for the Rector is
a person of mark and character; and you cannot
look upon his sincere and earnest face, without
feeling at once, that whatever counterfeits you
have seen elsewhere, here is a man wearing the
true image of the God he serves.

In stature he is about five feet eight inches;
and of a strong build. His hair and eyes are
black; and his features, though hard, are musically set. There is at times a comical shrewd-
ness about his face; and he is fond of a joke;
loving geniality and good fellowship; and rejoicing in troops of friends, who are never so
happy as when their legs are under his table, or
walking with him under the leafy colonades of
the beautiful park, in which the Rectory is situated. His age is about forty, and if I might
lease his life, he should live to be as old as
Abraham; for he is a good man, and knows the
high purposes of existence, which he seeks to
realize both in his public and private relations.

If the reader should happen to be a fastidious
and straight-laced person, he will perhaps be at
a loss to reconcile that tossing up of the hat,
which I have mentioned above, with my present
statement of the Rector's high principle and
inherent goodness. But depend upon it, Oh,
excellent reader! that the fault is in thee, and not
in him. I do not wish to be personal, but I love
honesty and truth; and would have the reader
consider this thing in his heart. For it is quite

true that the Rector likes his joke, and a wise merriment, without forgetting that he is a responsible man, and a servant of the living God. Nay, he even thinks that he serves God best by being happy himself, and making others happy, —a creed which one could wish were a little more general in its acceptation. Hence there never was a happier or a more beautiful home than his; and few men live with so many blessings, from so many, and such various persons, upon them. Indeed, he is a universal benefactor! The poor of his own village, the needy scholar, the exiled patriot, the unfortunate friend, are alike recipients of his bounty. Wherever a good work is going on, he is sure to have a hand in it; and thus, either by his purse or his counsel —or both united—aids its progress and completion. He reigns in his Valley of the Trent, like the lordly Sun in his heavens, a noble, hospitable, generous, and beautiful soul. Mark what a bland and sunny smile comes over his face every now and then; and if you are a good reader of the unwritten scroll of man's heart, you will know, by that gleam of light which flashes from within outwards, that it comes from a great and benevolent nature. And yet, strange as it may appear to the fastidious reader, the Rector rarely lets his humour escape in words; and were it not for the eyes, and a certain emotional twitching of the facial nerves, no one could tell, even in cases of tragic interest, that he was at all affected by them. He understands well enough what Carlyle means by *silence,* and more than that, he practises what the same writer teaches respecting *action.* He is a philanthropist, not of the closet merely, but in the wide signification of that term, on a large and cosmopolitan scale. He is allied by birth and family relations, to the highest ranks in English society; and yet he places himself upon an equality with the humblest artisan, and identifies himself with the popular interests. Not indiscriminately, however; for although he is charitable in his constructions of all actions, that will admit of a difference of opinion, he has deep-seeing eyes, and can read character at a glance; so that he is rarely, if ever, imposed upon in his judgments, or in his alliances. It is good and worthy men and causes, which he seeks and strives to aid; and he cares not a rush for what the world calls respectability and fashion. His fashion is the good old way of Paul, who went about to make *men* better. He loves *men,* and not the coats they wear, or the cellars, larders, and appurtenances, they may happen to possess. Humanity, indeed, is his religion; and his sermons —which he preaches every Sunday in the little church hard by—are as beautiful and affectionate as St. John's Gospel. How the old, patriarchal men and women of the village love him! and the little children look like flowers in the congregation—they are so happy, innocent, and smiling.

He is too good a man, however, not to have enemies; and I am sorry to say these spring mostly from the surplice. Shall I tell you why? Alas! he thinks and teaches, as Christ thought and taught, that all men are brethren; and that the heavenly love of Christianity should no longer be a name merely, but a vital and active principle, animating the world, and making all societies a reflex of its divinity and beauty. He thinks that Competition is a great social evil; the fruitful cause of want, misery, and crime; that it is the deadliest foe of Christian life and practice; the root of selfishness, pride, arrogance, and all the nameless, manifold, passions and iniquities which deface the moral and social aspect of the world. But what then, you ask, does he suggest to take the place of Competition? Are we not indebted to this principle of action for our present civilization—our trade, commerce, manufactures; even for our learning and Protestant religion? True, but our friend the Rector, who is a philosopher as well as a philanthropist, believes that Competition has had its day—that it has done its work;—that the Maker used it as an instrument to accomplish the stability of modern civilizations, and has now let go the handle, leaving it, by the very insanity of its guideless and godless operations, to become the further instrument of that noble reform, of which he is an old and distinguished advocate. But what is this reform? I hear you ask, with some little impatience. Simply this : that he who eats, shall work. He lays it down, as the first principle in his economy, that *all* ought to labour ; that no man, willing to work, should starve ; that no man should be allowed to starve ; that Capital ought no longer to eat up Industry ; that Industry ought no longer to be cheated out of its just rights, but share in the common production of wealth ; in short, that Co-operation should supercede Competition ; and that such societary arrangements ought to be made, that each should work for the good of all.

This may sound strangely enough to the ears of the fastidious reader, and he may be inclined to call the brave Rector by the somewhat cant names of "communist" and "visionary." The first he certainly is ; the latter he is not. For communion does not necessarily mean Owenism, and "community of women,"—for if it did, my friend, the Rector, would be the first man to send it to the right-about—but it means a noble union of interests, a heroic sacrifice of self to the good of the common weal. It is, moreover, a "great fact" that the tendencies of the age are towards this very communism, and that the highest men amongst us are, either by direct or indirect teaching, engaged in promulgating the ideas which will bring about this new epoch in human affairs.

I can imagine the fastidious reader preferring his "visionary" charge against the Rector in this matter; and I can also imagine the half-earnest, half-comical expression of the said Rector's face, as he listened to it. Be sure, good reader, that he would make you quite as much of a " visionary " as he is himself, before he had done with you, in such case. That is, supposing that you really had a soul in your body, which was not quite dead; quite choked with the doctrines of what is called " Political Economy," and the conventional ideas of society. And especially, if you claimed to be considered a *Christian*, there would be no hope of your escaping from this merciless and visionary Rector. For if Christianity be true—as I am foolish enough to hope and believe that it is—then our modern civilization, and all the laws, saws, and institutions upon which it is built, and of which it is composed, are false. Christianity commands us to love one another; and we show our love by getting all we can, on the principle of Competition, and coolly look on whilst our neighbour starves.

I will not enter into the question here, however, for this was not the purpose I proposed when I commenced writing; and I fear I have already gone a little too far out of my way, although I could not have given any idea of the Rector, if I had said less. As to the practical working of any Co-operative scheme, no wise man, I suppose, will at present pretend to give

B 3

an opinion; still less to propose a scheme in the hope of its fitting the world like a pair of breeches. It is enough to know that the *principle* of Co-operation is true; and that communism, in one form or other, is the inevitable shape which society must assume, in order to escape from its own Frankensteins, and the suicidal jaws of Capital and Machinery. The Rector believes, likewise, that Communism alone can develope the highest capabilities of humanity; and that to bring about this great epoch, all good men should lend a helping hand, by preparing the public mind for its coming.

Here, then, you have an outline of the Rector's person, character, and opinions. Can you wonder that my heart beat quickly at the thought of seeing him on that sunny day in June? or that our meeting was so warm and friendly?

But I had nearly forgotten the lady, who, on this occasion, joined us on the grassy lawn, under the shade of the great beech tree, and was so animated in her praises of Tennyson's new poem. She was of a tall and graceful person, and had the sweetest hazel eyes you ever saw; they were so clear, that you could look into the chambers of her soul, and read all its secrets of thought, beauty, and passion. Her hair was a dark brown, and her cheeks were tinged with a rosy, almost hectic colour, and told, I fear too sad a tale, of inward suffering. Her manners were fascinating, and her voice was like the music of a rivulet, full of gushes and sunshine. Her mind was as beautiful as her person; and she delighted in metaphysical discussion, and loved to break her sword over the Rector's shoulders. But the Poets were her best friends, and she knew them all by heart. You should have heard—or rather Tennyson should have heard—what she said of the "Princess," and of him. He is doubtless quite used to sweet words from the lips of beautiful women; but *hers* would have fallen on him like the breath of violets, and if they had not turned his head, I think—judging from myself—that they would at least have turned his heart. Well, there we lay, on the warm grass before the old Rectory windows, until it was time to go and dress for dinner. I preferred, however, to remain behind, for my toilette was complete for the day.

And here let me give you a sketch of this delightful retreat. The Rectory is an old-fashioned house, as I have before told you, with two large windows jutting out from the walls, one on either side the front door. Roses and jasmines are trained around them; and you can step from the chamber windows upon the leads of these parlour windows. The house is three stories high, and it is literally embosomed in trees, except in front, where the beautiful park scenery opens before you like an enchanted picture. The park itself belongs to Lord M———n, and is kept in most delightful order. The Hall of the noble lord is situated about a stone's throw from the Rectory, although you cannot see it for the trees. A short walk, however, under the gloomy pines to the *right* of the Rectory—that is, supposing you to stand with your back to the front door—will conduct you to it, —and a noble mansion it is. Hark! you may hear the dogs barking in their kennels, even now; and that, too, in spite of the rooks which are still cawing overhead.

The Rector's family and that of Lord M— are related, and live on the most friendly terms. Lady M. who is a beautiful and true-hearted woman, disputes the palm of goodness with her brother, the Rector; and, like him, rejoices in making every one happy around her. It is in the blood of these admirable people, and they cannot help it. If Adam and Eve had been made of such stuff, we should have had a different world to that we live in. As it is I only wonder—when I think about the apple; which *didn't* choke Eve, as it ought to have done— that so much good should still be left in the human heart, as shows itself here and there. However, I must not be caught in the meshes of this question of moral evil; although I am ashamed of the whole race of man because evil exists at all; and never could discover what business it has in so fine and moral a world. What has evil to do with the Rectory, and the people thereof, (for example,) I should like to know? I always picture this place and this people, as Eden and Edeners; and have no fear of another Eve to spoil it with her curious taste for apples. I will return, therefore, to my description of the locality.

To the left of the house, by a gravel walk—overhung with trees through which the sunlight never enters, and where it is always as cool as any hidden nook in the vales of Westmoreland—you ascend a natural terrace, about a mile and a half long, from which, through the open vistas of the trees, you catch glimpses of a glorious and almost boundless landscape. The terrace is sheltered with trees and shrubs, where the birds sing all day long, and the nightingale rings the starry air into music all the night. Rare flowers with their rich-coloured blossoms, and fiery petals—flash in the sunshine at your feet, as you pass along; and every now and then a tawny-legged hare, or a nimble rabbit, darts from the wood-cover; and crosses the terrace within a couple of yards of you, rushing down with a neck-break pace into the lowland pastures.

I cannot imagine a more beautiful walk than this, especially for lovers; and it is worth while to *fall* in love—notwithstanding the misery of that kind of *gravitation*—for the sake of trying it. Still, I don't know how it is, but I have very melancholy and yet beautiful association

with this terrace walk.   I suppose, I got them
from a picture painted by my friend W. B.
Scott, of Newcastle, (brother to the great David
Scott, artist, of Edinborough) which he sent me
some two years ago.   The picture represents a
pageantry of beautiful men and women, ad-
vancing in pairs, up a gloomy terrace, over-
arched with trees; like that I have just described.   There is a mystic solemnity about the
figures, which strikes you in spite of the gaiety
of their step.   Some are just appearing with
their heads above the terrace, as if they came
from an unknown country—others are seen in
the full pride of manhood and womanhood in the
middle of the walk—others on the summit of the
hill—and still farther on, others are hurrying
down into the unknown country, from whence
they all came.   You can see the deep azure of
the sky, at the extremity of the terrace, and the
large white stars; and that is all.   The picture
is called " *Whither go they? An Enigma;*" the
most striking and mystic picture I have ever seen.
Well, I think it must be the fusing in my
mind of this picture with the terrace walk at
B——, which makes me have such sad, and yet
pleasing associations, with it. Be this as it may,
and maugre my own feelings, the terrace is a
walk which one never forgets; and as I said, a
pair of lovers, (who had not seen " *Whither go
they? An Enigma;*") might be as happy under
those gorgeous old trees—in the presence of that

fine landscape—and in the midst of all those
flowers and singing-birds, as —— kissing can
make them.

Now you must imagine dinner to be over; for
I dislike writing of fish, flesh, and fowl, however much I may relish them in the eating.
After dinner, however, things begin to look a
little more poetical. There is the wine, for instance; a liquid lyric in itself; especially if it
be Burgundy; for this to my taste, is the Anac-
reon of all vintages. Formerly I liked Port,
and despised lighter wines—your Champagnes,
Clarets, Hocks, Hermitages—as fit nourishment
for fairies and women. And even now, when
Burgundy is not to be had, I prefer the noble
and generous blood of my ruddy friend, to the
chilly white-blooded wines which have become
so fashionable of late. It is a brave sight, a
decanter of good Port!

I think Bacchus is belied when he is represented as getting drunk on raw grapes: and I
doubt, indeed, whether he ever got drunk at all
on those light wines of Greece and Rome. If
the jolly god had been acquainted with the
virtues of our illustrious Port, the case would
have been different, and the fact somewhat par-
donable. Even Socrates—strong-stomached and
hard-headed a fellow as he was—who could
drown the Mediterranean-throat of Alcibiades,
and coolly drink out all the guests at Plato's
Banquets—nothing injured by these deep liba-

tions, but as much of a man in the morning, after
he had washed his head at the public fountain,
as he was before he began to drink, the night
before—even Socrates I say, would not have got
off so easily, if he had been drinking Port, instead
of that sweet musty compound, which the Greeks
nicknamed by calling it wine.

But it is precisely on account of the potent
influence of this mighty Giant of the Sun—
whose locks drop with rubies, and whose odor-
ous breath steals away one's senses, as if by
enchantment—that I am compelled to forswear
him, and pass by on the other side of his sorce-
ries.   It is the fault of my stomach, however,
and not because I dislike the seductive charms
of this old jovial Titan ; and I make this confession as a matter of justice to an old friend, whom
the fates oblige me to abandon. I like the colour
of him, however, so well, that I have adopted
his younger brother, whom men call Burgundy.
Not that this is his real Christian name—for
Christianity in these teetotal days, has all but
struck Paul himself from the calendar of her
saints, heroes, and martys, for recommending
Timothy to take a little wine for his stomach's
sake :—Christianity, therefore, has nothing to
do with Burgundy—and his name was given to
him by heathen (that is to say, Bacchanalian)
godfathers.   Nevertheless, he is a fine fellow !
and " my delight of a shiny night," after dinner
—especially at the Rectory, where they dine at

7 o'clock, p. m.,   Indeed, without the aid of this good friend, I cannot understand how the gastric juices could get through the work of digestion before bed-time; and I prefer Burgundy to nightmares.

Well, look around you, good reader; for although the sight to you must unhappily be Barmecidal—yet to me who partook of the fare, on the occasion in question, it was very far from that.   Look around you, I say, and behold a noble palatial board, groaning under the weight of wines, fruits, and flowers: for flowers are always in season, and set off a table almost as beautifully as fair women—to whom, indeed, they are related—as I have heard Flora and Venus declare, although I could never learn by what secret of crossing and breeding the relationship came about.

Here, however, we not only have flowers, but women also; fit to adorn a divine symposium. There is the Rector's lady, at the end of the table, opposite her husband; a quiet and serene mother, with all her blooming boys and girls around her.   She, kind soul! is helping them to the good things on the table; and there is one chubby little Cupid, with blue eyes, and flaxen hair, who has set his white teeth into an orange, despising the silver knives and plates, as if they were really an absurd invention.   See, what faith the rogue has in his teeth and fingers!   The remonstrances of the fair Mater are all in vain, to this real son of Adam and Eve—for what does *he* care about etiquette? The rest of the children are quite as busy as he; but more orderly, and have respect unto the decencies of the table. On the right hand of the Rector, is our beautiful friend, whom we met a while ago in the garden; and here am I, on the left— where the wicked are destined to be—only I do not feel wicked just now; for the moral atmosphere of this banquetting-room, and the exhilirating influence of the Burgundy, make me feel as much like a god, (heathen god, of course) as a poor mortal can ever hope to feel. Do not think, however, that we lost time in all this eating and drinking, or that either was carried to excess. Excess of any sort is an evil thing; and takes the pay out of you beside, which is not pleasant. For no man likes to pay—not even his debts—and therefore, I take this as an admonishment on the part of Nature that we should keep the debtor and creditor sides of our life square and even;—in other words, that we should not get into debt at all. A thing, by the way, much easier to preach than practise! No excess was committed by us, however; and the sensuality of our repast, (for all repasts *are* sensual, according to the saints—whom, may God forgive!—inasmuch as they do not believe in the human kitchen) the sensuality of our repast I say, was relieved and redeemed by a conversation upon certain

high topics, which I have no time to repeat
here.

When the ladies retired to the drawing-room,
and the children were sent to the nursery to
prepare for bed, the Rector and I sat down by
the window, looking out over the lawn and
garden, upon the undulating scenery of the
park, as it lay stretched before us in the deep-
ening shadows of the twilight. Here we talked
of old friends, whom I had often met at the
Rectory, in times long past, and pledged them
all in right good bumpers, wishing they were
then present with us. By some chance or other,
I happened to allude to Sherwood Forest, and
the Rector expressed a wish to see that fine old
realm of ruin and desolation. I told him that
nothing would give me greater pleasure than to
accompany him there ; and, indeed, seeing that
the weather was so settled and beautiful, I
suggested that we should make up a party on
the morrow, and have a day of it. The good
Rector instantly fell in with the idea, and as the
servant came just then to announce that the
ladies were waiting tea for us in the drawing
room, away we went, to reveal our project to
them ; and had the pleasure to find that it met
with their entire approval and concurrence.

The number of ladies had been increased, since
dinner, to four ; and I was now introduced to
the Hon. Miss M——, who had come in, with her
fair governess, to spend the evening. Miss M——

was a slight and beautiful creature, about seventeen years old; pale as marble, with dark eyes and hair; and of a gentle, confiding, and most affectionate nature. She was as graceful as a fawn, both in her person and motions; her hands were small and white (and it is a rare thing, mark you! to see a beautiful hand—which indeed belongs to breeding, and is the only sign of blood, which, as Byron says, aristocracy can generate). And then her feet——shall I describe her feet? I think it is Suckling who has written a couplet about a lady's feet, in which he describes them as like "little mice," peeping in and out from the folds of the fair one's dress. And, oddly enough, this figure of the mice hits the case exactly, and represents the eternal peeping of a pair of pretty feet, better than any other figure I can think of.—Such, then, is an outline of the Hon. Miss M—. Add to which, that her manners were sweet, winning, and simple. There was no affectation about her; nothing to make you feel her rank, or warn you from honest speech in that presence; but she was bland, generous, modest, and unassuming, in all that she said or did. She reminded me of what Nature must have thought about when she made flowers; for she was a flower set to music.

Her governess was a merry, intelligent lady, of small stature, and full, rounded proportions. Her complexion was fair and fresh-coloured, her hair brown, and her eyes were dark, large, and bright, covered with long black lashes, and flashing upon you with a dangerous beauty. I can speak for myself, at all events, in this case, and confess that those splendid eyes haunt me at this moment, as vividly as if I had only just felt their power.

Well, it was resolved by this conclave of beautiful persons (I do not include the Rector and myself here, although *he*, at least, was very far from being a Cyclop) that we should make up a party the next day for Sherwood; and it was further resolved to call at the house of a good Quaker friend of mine (who lived lower down in the valley, about six miles off), and invite him to accompany us. Accordingly, the party separated at an early hour, to prepare themselves, by a good night's rest, for the fatigue of the following day. The Rector and I, however, had more things to talk about before we went up to our beds; besides, he knew that I was very partial to a cigar, and he could not think of sending me to rest without suffering me to indulge my propensity. Fortunately, the Rector had just received a case of Manillas, from a friend in Ceylon; and upon trial I found them " choicely good," as Izaak Walton says. After all, however, there is nothing like an Havanna, for breadth and flavour. Manillas I could not stick to, because of the opium with which they are saturated; Bulwer or Tennyson

might ;—(both being great smokers ; the former
an opium-eater, and smoker, of long standing ;
and the latter a tobacco-smoker, which he burns
in a short black clay pipe ;) I say, both these
poets might adopt the Manilla with advantage ;
that is, if I may judge of them, by the feelings
I experience whilst indulging in these Eastern
dream-makers. For I have lived, at such times,
with "*Zanoni*" and the "*Lotus-eaters*," and seen
likewise more glorious visions than anything
represented in these books. The hint is worth
considering perhaps ; and more especially by
poets who cannot persuade the *divine* afflatus to
move them. As for the rest of the tribe of
cigars, I make very little account of them. A
first-rate English Havanna, however, is not to
be despised—except by the aristocracy, who
like to pay two guineas a pound for a *foreign*
article, because it *is* foreign. It is true that
there is a flavour—a rich, indescribable, tropical
flavour—in a foreign cigar, which no English
maker can equal ; and the reason is, that the leaf
loses its aroma in the process of manufacture ;
for it has to be damped afresh before it can be
made up, and exhalation steals the aforesaid
flavour away. Nevertheless, enough of the real
virtue of the leaf still remains, to give me, at
all events, a sufficient satisfaction. Formerly, I
used to smoke Yara cigars, but I have now become an epicure, (if I smoke cigars at all, which
is a rare case with me, for I prefer my noble

meerschaum instead,) and can no longer relish the soft, sweet, Yara flavour. A mixture of Yara and Havanna, with a Columbia wrapper, is more to my taste; but I hate the dry, stinking odour of the German tobacco, and wonder how my transcendental friends can write books on it. It must be a scabby soil that of Germany; and very ungrateful to boot, or it would afford a better plant for such fine fellows as the Germans are. Latakia, and Syrian, are the best of all Eastern tobaccos; although they are apt to leave a stinging sensation in the palate.—Hence I always smoke a rough-cut Cuba tobacco, which is as smooth as cream, although full-flavoured enough to satisfy the most seasoned brother of this universal smoke-guild, which the world has of late become.

Behold us then, (said Rector and myself) seated before the kitchen fine! and I pray you, O fastidious reader! do not turn up your nose at the thought of it. For, after all, unless there be a smoke-room in the house of your friend, the kitchen is the most suitable place to turn a smoking guest into. And the reason is that ladies (to their shame be it spoken) are not fond of the odour of tobacco; although, acccording to my nostrils, it beats hollow all their incense pastilles, and *Eau de Cologne!* Besides which, there is a sort of do-what-you-like air about a good, large, comfortable kitchen, especially at night, when the household is gone to rest, and the fire blazes up the capacious chimney, and only you and your friend, or friends, are present, to enjoy it. How friendly, and homely too, the chairs and tables look ! They seem to say, "Take your ease, gentlemen ! Don't be afraid of making us serve you ; we are used to it. We are not like those fine, dandy fellows in the drawing-room, with their gilt frames and satin backs—fit only for our dear young ladies to sit on ;—for look you ! we are solid and substantial boys, that wouldn't shrink at a man weighing sixteen stone avoirdupoise !" And the jolly fellows stare at you with honest eyes, all the while : just ready, in appearance, to slap their oaken sides by way of emphasis. Well, in this hearty company—watched by the laughing faces of innumerable brass kettles and saucepans, which hung over the chimney wall, and by the grave looks of blue and white plates and dishes—arranged like so many epicurean judges above the long and well-scoured dresser—I say in this hearty and motley company did we two wile away the midnight—talking of endless things and persons,—from Jack Ketch and his strangling mission upon God's merciful and beneficent earth—to Charles Fourier and his scheme of Attractive Labour. At last we condescended to go to bed—because, as Mahomet said of the mountain—the bed would not come to us.

My dreams that night were strangely peopled with hangmen and fair women, Fourier and

Sherwood Forest ; and when I was getting right cozy between the sheets—(which "smelt of lavender," as Walton thinks they always should, in country houses), I was roused by the apparition of the Rector, who stood by my bedside in his dressing-gown, calling upon me with Stentorian lungs to *turn out*. Shall I speak the truth? I wished him at the unmentionable fellow's at that moment ; for it seemed to me that I had only just *turned in*. However, there was no help for it, as we had to start by eight o'clock ; so I arose to dress myself.

It was a fine, bright morning, and I opened the casement to let in the sunshine. Oh, how I enjoyed the rich draught of Heaven, which God sent me on the wings of the morning ! The dew lay wet upon the grass on the lawn, and the woods were dripping with beads of moisture, which reflected the rays of the glorious sun, and made the leaves sparkle like diamonds. Far away, in the park, grazed the sheep and oxen ; and I could see their fiery breath circling round them in wreaths of lurid smoke. The garden literally steamed with odours ; and the flowers were struggling with their fair faces to kiss the sunbeams once more. How I wished they had human sense and feeling, that I might kiss *them*—especially the roses ; for I love roses ; and always think of black eyes and hair ; sweet blushing cheeks, and bosoms of divine depth

c

and beauty, whenever I see them. The common rose—impiously nicknamed "'Cabbage-rose"—and the "*Moss-rose*," are my favourites; and in the summer time my pockets are sure to be half full of these beautiful dead creatures: for I always keep them till their bloom is quite gone, and then, I don't like to throw them away,—because I really love them, and believe that "a thing of beauty is a joy for ever."

Close to my window, our old friends, the rooks, were busy feeding their young, and cawing as loudly as ever,—a sure sign that they, at least, had had enough sleep, and were alive and well this morning. I was glad to see the dusky rogues, notwithstanding the trick they played me the day before; so I amused myself with singing a song to their honour, which I found amongst the beautiful lyrics scattered through the pages of "Festus"—the most wonderful poem ever written. The song begins thus :—

"The crow! the crow! the old black crow,"

and tells you how long the rascal lives, and how he loves the "fat meadows," and dines in a row,

"With his fifty black cousins, all black as a sloe,
   Crow, crow, you old black crow !"

Says the chorus,—

"It's jolly to live like an old black crow."

And in this way I amused myself and the rooks, until I was ready to go down to breakfast.

I found the Rector's lady and her children at table, when I went into the room, and after mutual congratulations I sat down to enjoy the coffee and toast, and cold fowl, ham, and all the endless things which the hospitable board, and the sweet words of the good Mater, invited me to partake of. Presently our lady friend—she of the garden and "Princess," I mean,—made her appearance; her eyes all too bright, and her cheeks flushed as with the kisses of Aurora. She smiled when she entered, wished us good morning, and took her seat beside the Mater. But you should see her smile, to know what a smile is; and all I could tell you about the musical curve of her lips, and the pearly teeth they reveal, when the sunshine of her heart gushes over her face in that way, would give you no idea of it. And then her voice—but it is of no use getting into ecstacies; so we will say no more about it. By and by, the Rector came dropping into the room. He had been ordering the coachman to be punctual with the carriage; and the mouthful of air he got whilst executing this mission, gave him the appetite of a wolf.

Precisely at eight o'clock the carriage drove up to the door, and whilst we were arranging our caps, coats, and provisions, the Hon. Miss M——, and the governess, made their appearance up the avenue of pines, leading from the hall, accompanied by a servant in livery, who carried their cloaks, shawls, and etceteras. In a few minutes we were all seated, and the carriage drove off. I thought as we passed the kennel, where the Newfoundland dog was chained, that the poor fellow would have died with grief to see us go away without him. He jumped at his chain, barked, howled, and when he saw it was of no use, laid down with his head upon his fore paws, and whined so pitiously that I could have given my ears to have set him at liberty. I knew, however, that we should have had him shot if we took him with us to the Forest. And so I consoled myself with the reflection that we were doing him a kindness in leaving him behind.

The horses dragged us up the steep hill, leading to the Cliffe Road, in fine style, and we were soon fairly on our journey. The free, bracing air, made the party very joyous and communicative; and almost sent me mad. For it is singular enough, and yet true,—as all my friends can testify—that air, sunshine, and fine scenery, have an effect upon my spirits equal to the most glorious inspirations of my beloved Burgundy, and far more healthy, because more natural. I cannot hold myself on such occasions; but my spirit goes forth to embrace the landscape, and the immeasureable blue sky, with infinite yearnings, and seems to clasp them with its everlasting arms, in an infinite embrace. I forget all con·

ventionalities at such times, (and indeed, at most times ; for my nature is impulsive, and abhors restraint,) and yield myself up entirely to the influences of earth and heaven. On this occasion, I was quite uproarous—and although I did not swear—like the Englishman in "Hyperion," and damn the Saint Wolfgang of the valley, in the very exuberance of excited joy,— I fear it was not the *law*, but the *ladies*, that prevented me. For somehow or other, oaths often come into my mouth (like base counters, as they are,) when I mean to pray, and be thankful : and many a time have I passed them, quite unconsciously, for blessings ! How comes it, this profanity, in the sacred presence of Nature ? I cannot defend it, much less fathom it ; and leave it, therefore, to be resolved by the doctors of psychological science.

How beautiful it was, as we rattled over the sound, hard road, to watch the glorious landscape of the Trent Valley, as it lay far below us, with its villages, farms, woodlands, streams, and pastures,—a wide and boundless landscape, losing itself in the dim mists of the horizon. I never pass that way without thinking of Macauley's ballad of the "Spanish Armada," in which he represents the great bell—"Old Tom," he is called—of Lincoln, giving the alarm of the dreaded invasion, and swinging its ponderous numbers "o'er all the Vale of Trent."

c 3

Civilization has altered its face a little since those Elizabethian times—when Shakspere and Ben Johnson made plays, and audiences listened to them at ten o'clock in the morning; and the Queen drank her quart of beer, and ate her pound of beef to breakfast—rising with the cock! And notwithstanding that the poets, and the humanity-men, mourn over the decay of those " good old times," I think we have gained so much more than they were ever worth (always excepting the unknown and immeasureable worth of gentle Willy, and the galaxy of poets and statesmen, and discoverers, which revolved round him as their centre) that we can very well afford to let them remain buried—with all the good and evil things of the times that are past. To say nothing of what commerce and manufactures, iron and steam, and the steam press have done for us, only think what a privilege it is to travel at this bountiful rate, on this Cliffe Road—with a certain prospect of arriving —barring accidents—at Sherwood Forest, in the space of three hours at the most! In those " good old times," it would have taken us two days; for the Elizabethian carriages were nothing but stage-waggons, gilt and painted; and the Elizabethian roads were execrable for mud and highwaymen. Certainly, Robin Hood was no longer a denizen of the wold and forest, nor was there any fear of his " merry men," and their quarter staves; but the " forty-eighth," or ninth, of Elizabeth, I forget which, had not withdrawn vagabonds from the roads, nor thieves either; hence our carriage would have had to bristle with loaded firelocks—and we to be accoutred wth broadswords and the "bull-dogs" that bark and bite, without any living organism of throat and jaws.

Glory to Queen Victoria, the Police, and—shall I say so? to the Public Morals; here we are, without warlike weapons to defend ourselves with, except the bright eyes in the carriage behind us—and without fear, save that of losing our hearts—which is not quite so bad as losing our lives, at the instance of the Elizebethian highwaymen. But do listen how the owners of those bright eyes are laughing and talking; and behold how the beautiful and quiet Mater en-joys, to the very depths of her serene soul, the happiness of these caged and merry birds.

And now, good Rector, give me your hand, and let us congratulate ourselves upon this glo-rious cup of joy, which we have stolen from the grip of the black and moody Fates. Ah me! if all life were such an easy journey as this (says one side of the Janus-face of man) how we should thank God for it. Perhaps not (says the grave, reflective side of the same old Janus-face) for then I fear we should not enjoy life at all—and so end in upbraiding God that he had made so bad an experiment in his world. For I see tha if a man would enjoy a pleasure, he must know how to bear a pain—he must earn his holiday by hard work. And to this I (who am Janus himself) very heartily subscribe. What say you, young ladies? "Give you as much happiness, and as little misery, as possible?" Well, that is precisely what I say; only we will earn the happiness first. I suppose if Epicurus and Solon were now teaching at Athens, you would join the school of the former; and, notwithstanding the lies that have been told about Epicurus, I am not sure that you are not right. Solon was a little crabbed in his love for the Absolute Truth, and did not give the senses fair play.— Nay, he confessed at the "Banquet of the Seven Sages," held at Corinth, under the Presidency of Periander, that he, for his part, could not see the use of a stomach, except to plague the owner of it, and advised all men to live as though the said stomach were not. Now, I like, as you do, the gardens, and statuary, the flowers, and fountains, and singing-birds, in the midst of which Epicurus taught—and the simple but plentiful banquets, and the pleasant and innocent recreations he enjoined— far better than the godlike sourness and indifference to such things, which Solon manifested in his life and discourses. I don't want to philosophise or to preach, in such a holiday as this, (and we will drop the subject directly; only, now that I have begun, it will be as well to finish gracefully)—but trust me for once, as an interpreter of Nature in her human designs, that it is only by the harmonious play and balance of all the faculties, that we can become true and complete persons. I am glad you concur in this statement, most excellent Rector! And now, coachman, take care, and don't break your horses' knees in going down this hill. For we must turn off here, and journey, for awhile, on the old Roman road, which runs from Lincoln, and crosses the Cliffe, at this point, on its way to Littleborough Ferry.

The road is now called Till-bridge-lane; and the village of Scampton lies away to the right of us—owned, with all the adjoining lands for some thousands of acres, by Sir George Kayley, Bart. It is singular that this village has made little or no progress, in extent or population, since Doomsday Book! The land is tied up by the law of entail, and Sir George won't allow the poor to breed upon it, lest they should become chargeable thereon. Hence he sends them away, at such times, to the neighbouring parishes; and some of his labourers, I hear, come from Lincoln every morning, and go back foot-weary at night, to return next morning, and so on till death. God help them!

My friend, the Quaker—whose little hamlet of B. we shall soon discern in the landscape, and whose honest hand I long to lay hold of,—had a regular fight about five years ago with Sir George's steward, at an auction, which took place at the aforesaid hamlet,—a fight, I say, to see who should buy a lot of miserable cottages, which Sir George wanted as a warren for his labourers to breed in ! The iniquity of the thing lay in Sir George's endeavouring to free his own estate of its just burdens, and palm them upon my Quaker friend; for, as the law then stood, the parish where children were born was obliged to support them. The wickedness of the attempt was defeated by the public spirit of the Quaker, (and honour to thee for it, brave Tom ! say I,) although he had to pay hundreds of pounds for property that was scarcely worth two hundred. Never mind about that now, however; for the transaction is over—although, I confess, the memory of it is a little offensive to the nostrils of a good man.

The Scampton estates are well cultivated, and the labourers that live upon them—about twelve I believe—have good cottages, gardens, and a few acres of land between them, upon which they grow their wheat, barley, and potatoes. This is as it should be; and if all labourers were as well provided for, instead of every eighth or ninth person in England being a pauper, we should have no paupers. And such a state of things would delight your heart, good Rector ! would'nt it ? However, " God will mend all; or by God, Donald ! we must help him to mend it ;" I don't know which, precisely. In the meanwhile, an interesting fact remains to be told about Scampton; for dull as it looks, and little as it has progressed since the making of Dooms-day Book, in Norman William, the Conqueror's time, it was once a place of considerable note; although the time of its noteriety was long anterior to William the Conqueror,— and whilst his piratical ancestors were cutting each other's throats at home, or those of other people, in their Viking expeditions, on the Norwegian seas abroad. In short, it was a Roman station, and this Till-bridge-lane was, as I said, the old Roman Road. I remember some seven years ago, being shewn a beautiful tessellated pavement which was discovered in the heart of this ancient Villa (turned up by the plough;) and notwithstanding that the rich mosaic work was built over, in order to preserve it from destruction, the present Goth who farms the land upon which it was found, has converted the building (which ought to have been sacred to this interesting memorial of the great Roman conquerors and civilizers of Britain) into a shed for his cattle! and the last time I was that way, there were only a few broken and disjointed squares of the pavement left. Drive away, coachman! however, and let Scampton stand still for another thousand years, if the people will let it. For my part, I am heartily ashamed of the rule that obtains there; and think ten thousand acres ought to have more than thirty or forty household fires upon them.

See young ladies! we are now fairly in the valley—one of the richest in England. And mark, how waving and beautiful, the long grass of the meadows, and the green crops of corn appear. As far as your bonny bright eyes can see, the whole expanse is cultivated, and blooming with verdure. It is not a picturesque landscape, however,—that is, to a mountaineer; although I confess to like the boundless flat which it presents, as a change and contrast to my own dark hills round Huddersfield. I like to see too, how Nature balances herself in these hills and dales as she goes up and down the world; for she is a cunning old lady, and is up to the laws—which she never violates, notwithstanding her antics. These overhanging trees too, and thick hedges which grow by the roadside—with the bright galaxies of flowers which shine amid the grass, on the banks, and lie in the hedge bottoms—and these merry birds that sing to us all the way, and never weary—are not they beautiful? Beautiful? Yes. And the azure sky above us—spread out like an infinite blue dome over a Cathedral world, dedicated to God and Love—how glorious it is! Look up, sweet maidens! You can almost see into Heaven.

Oh! I have looked up there, many and many a time, my spirit floated away into those boundless, fathomless floods of ether, until I could almost hear the music of God's garment as it trailed over the spangled pavement of the immeasurable universe, whilst sounds which no tongue could utter, and visions which no pen or pencil could describe, smote upon my wildered brain, and drove me—like the flaming swords of Eden—back, sorrowfully back to earth.— Now, would you not like to uplift that mighty curtain—which hides the immortal, the invisible and infinite—from your dark and beautiful eyes?   Oh! I know you would, or you would belie your descent from that curious grandam of yours and mine, who did so much mischief in Eden.   Here, however, we are at Till-bridge; and there to the right is the old fashioned inn, "*The Red Lion,*" with its swing sign board, dangling like a dead man on a gallows tree.   I like that inn, and the people that live in it too; for I was once kindly entertained there—many years ago,—eleven at least—when I came down to look after a school (advertized to trap unfortunate scholars into starvation), which I got and kept for eighteen months, living great part of the time on oatmeal and water, and envying the vile pigs the milk, which the good farmers would not *sell* me; (I, not being so valuable as a pig, because they could not turn me into bacon and eat me, for I am naturally a wiry, bony fellow, like one of Pharaoh's lean kine) I say I envied these pigs the milk which the farmers *gave* them.   But thereby hangs a tale; some-

D

thing more tragical than a pig's *tail*, even when
the butcher has done with him.   Yet I do not
regret the experience I bought at this place
(Sturton village, by Stowe, is the name of it;
and you see the "*school house*," where I taught
and starved, on the left; as you come from Lincoln to Gainsborough) but would gladly go
through it all again, if I had to begin life
afresh.   For had I not starved at Sturton, I
should never have known my Quaker friend—
who lives at the next hamlet, just over the pastures—(but we shall see him directly) and a
true friend, and a most royal soul, would have
been lost to me for ever.   We will leave the
"Red Lion," however, with its flower garden
—full of sweet peas, thyme, marjoram, gilly
flowers, lad's love, roses, and lavender—and
cross the bridge, underneath which runs the
Till; a stream fed by a lake many miles
higher up, and flowing into the Fosdyke near
Saxelby.   I have some very delightful memories
of that old Till, and know every inch of it, even
to the rat-holes, from the Bridge to the Foss.—
During my residence in this neighbourhood, I
used to spend most of my leisure time by the
banks of this stream.   For you must know that
I was a fisherman, and loved the sunny meadows through which the Till flows, quite as
well as the fishing which lured me to those sweet
and flowery solitudes.   Not that I have any
compunctions of conscience about killing fish;

for I am one of those old-fashioned people who believe that fish were made to be caught; and as to the cruelty of the sport, why, as quaint old Ben Franklin says, since the rascals catch and eat one another, I don't see why I should not catch and eat them. Besides which, fish are the greatest thieves and gormandizers in creation. You cannot drop a harmless bait into the water, but they must come and steal it; and as the law of retribution extends even to the finny tribe—and lower down indeed, to the very rudiments of life—the hook is the punishment which they get for their felony;—they are *caught* in the act. I was never fond of angling, however; not because I was frightened at Dr. Johnson's definition of an angler—viz., "a worm at one end of a line, and a fool at the other;" but because this method of fishing was too slow and wearisome to me. I did my work upon a larger scale, and went forth to kill the sharks of our fresh-water streams; that is, I was a pike-fisher, and have taken between forty and fifty pounds in a day.

I used to rise early in the Summer mornings—often with the sun—and go down Saxelby-lane, past Inglewood and Saxelby wood, on my way to the little bridge which crosses the Till near Saxelby village, close to the "*Steam Engine*," and commence fishing for bait—such as dace, roach, and even perch (for I have killed many a noble pike with perch, after cutting off the devil's wing on the top of their backs); and when I had caught as many fish as I wanted for bait, I used to take out my trimmers, one by one, with their long brass hooks, and having duly prepared them, drop them into the shallows all down the stream, or into deep holes, which I had cut with a sickle amongst the weeds. Then, whilst the trimmers were in the water, I had nothing to do but eat my breakfast, read, wander about, and smoke. And many beautiful things I saw at such times, by that old stream, and amongst those bright meadows, I can tell you. But I never caught Nature asleep, although I have seen her drowsy enough, to all appearance; and when I would have plucked the jewels from her ears, behold! she was a-tiptoe, and off.

I loved those early-risings, and think of them now with pleasure; and the more so, because I never get out of bed, in this degenerate town life which I live, until the Sun comes in and laughs at me, through my chamber windows.—— But you cannot think how pleasant and exciting it was, as I passed down Saxelby-lane, with my rush basket, suspended by the fishing-rod, over my shoulder. I scarcely knew the old world again in those dim and solemn mornings. The mist enveloped all the landscape with its vapoury garments, and the farm-houses loomed mysteriously through it, as if they were spellbound by Loke, and his Scandinavian imps, who wage mischievous war for ever, with the Sun and all the gods. Then there were the shadowy trees, waving their ghostly arms over me as I passed along; and every now and then the rooks, startled at my approach, would rise cawing from their roosts, and shake the dew-drops into my face, from their black and glossy wings. The bang of the gates, too, through which I had to pass; what a strange sound it was! And the cows and horses that came to look at me, with friendly faces, their necks half over the hedges, and their shaggy coats dripping with moisture, glad to see a human being afoot at that hour;—how the memory of all this sticks to me, like a picture! And then, when the sun arose, what a grand sight it was to behold the mists gradually roll away—like the smoke of a burnt-up world—whilst the blue and laughing heavens shone forth in their beauty and joyousness! I remember, too, as soon as the sun appeared, what an infinite number of rainbows danced over the dewy cobwebs, which the black-bearded spiders had woven all over the hedges. And as I sat upon the banks of the stream in the dewy stillness of the morning, I made acquaintance with the rats, weazels, and moor-hens, which haunted the Till; and with several species of dragon-flies, butterflies, and insects. The dragon-fly is a special favourite of mine, and I regard him as the king of insects. What a graceful, beautiful fellow he is! with his taper body stained with deepest purple, his head set in emeralds, his eyes like black diamonds, and and his long gauze wings stretching in double rows over his matchless shoulders. And then what a trumpet he blows!

By the way, talking of trumpets reminds me of the rich and varied tones which I have often heard in the insect world, especially on the sedgy margin of rivers, by the side of deep pools, and in the silence and solitude of shady woods. Many a time have I sat down on the grass, to listen to the concert which these little winged musicians were singing; and as often have I wondered, what lesson they intended to convey to me in their pipings. Did it never strike you, good Rector! that there is a deal of sorrow in the fact of our not being able to solve the mystery and economy of our dumb neighbours—or rather our sweet inarticulate neighbours—the birds and insects? to say nothing of the noble race of horses, and the calm Brahminical cows. In good faith, I declare I would not object to begin my existence in the lowest rudiments of Nature, so that I might grow into a thinking man at last (and as much higher in the scale of possible existence as you like); provided only, that I might remember the experiences and secrets of my former states, and preserve the faculty of speaking to every reptile, insect, bird, beast, and fish, in its own *patois*. I don't know how you feel, young ladies, but I am ashamed of myself when I go abroad into the fields and woods, to think what a dunce I am in the presence of so many beautiful living creatures, of whose ways and feelings I have no knowledge.

It was but last week (Whitsuntide), that I was in the vale of Cleveland, on my way to Rosebury-Topping, and having gathered a bunch of violets and blue-bells, in the wood, at the foot of the house where Captain Cook spent many of the earliest years of his valuable life, I took the charming nosegay with me to the top of that cone-like hill; and whilst I, and the friend who was with me, smoked our pipes and re-freshed ourselves at the fountain on the hill top, a music-laden, honey-laden, humble-bee came and rifled the blossoms and petals of the flowers which were lying on the grass at my feet. He was a gorgeous fellow; with belts of gold clasped round the black velvet mantle which Nature had arrayed him in; and he came with so much nonchallance to suck the sweets from my posy—that I saw he was merely doing his legitimate errand—that in short he was follow-ing his business. But although I asked him all manner of questions, viz. :—Where he came from? What he was doing, rambling about here, in sight of the North Sea, almost within hailing distance of the gullets of the Tees? What family he had at home? What religion he believed in? and where he expected to die

when he went to? I could get no other answer
than an angry, almost surly, musical buzzing.
Now, just think how pleasant it would have been
if I could have had half an hour's gossip with
this wild rover of the heath and mountains, *in
his own lingo!* What curious revelations he
would have made; and what a delightful book
might have been written about his rambles. I
would give much to know what he thinks of
this universe—of man and the starry heavens.
No doubt he would enlighten us a good deal, if
he could speak. Not, perhaps, that he has any
particular theories of man and the universe to
propound, although I have no doubt he has his
own way of thinking about *bees* and the universe; and if I might judge from his everlasting
piping, and his busy habits, I should say *his*
theory at least is reduced to practice; and that
it consists in making labour a real joy and
pleasure. I wonder Charles Fourier did not
place the Humble-Bee at the head of his
Phalansteries.

I must give up this random talk, however;
for here we are within sight of B——; and yonder red-tiled house, amongst the trees, is my
Quaker friend's house; and mine too, whenever
I like to take possession of it. "Which is the
house?" do you ask, my bonny damsels! Well,
rise up, and look for yourselves. There away,
right amongst the trees, as I said before. It is
the residence of a man, and not a journeyman;

which is a great thing to say, in these apish days. I have known him now these nine years, and have never met with a better man. I owe much to him, likewise, in the way of discipline and guidance. When I first became acquainted with him, I was all-but an atheist; was struggling with mental difficulties, and sorrows of the spirit, compared with which, those of "Werter" were mere comedy. From my sixteenth year, and earlier, I was left alone in the world, to battle with the mighty problems of life, death, and immortality, without a friend, counsellor, or guide. I was, moreover, in real earnest about the matter; a hater of lies, and a very Quixote in the pursuit of truth. But, alas! all my lances were broken against phantoms; and Truth herself fled away from me, as if in mockery. I could find no rest, from the crown of my head to the sole of my foot; and wandered about with my dark-lanthern and sword, ready and willing to find God, and fight the devil. But all my efforts were vain. The devil was always at hand; and, to do him justice, took what thrusts I gave him with very good humour, returning to the conflict unhurt, and with a horrible mocking laugh upon his face. But God, and the peace and blessedness of communion with Him, I could nowhere find. The earth revealed Him not, in its glory and beauty; and the sorrowful heavens shut down upon me like a dome

D 3

of brass. I read, thought, meditated, prayed, and at last despaired. "There is no God," I said; "or if there be, He is gone a hunting." For I spoke in the bitterness of a broken and desolate heart, and the words of Elijah the prophet, came to me as I have quoted them.

I spoke of my difficulties, and painful agonisings of spirit, to ministers and laymen; I argued with them, hoping to be convinced that I was wrong; but they all shrank from me after the first encounter, and denounced me as an infidel! I knew very well that I was an infidel; but how to be a Christian, without sacrificing my reason to the shrine of Religion, was what I most wanted to know; for infidelity was no pleasant meadow to dwell in; especially to me: for I was brought up after the strictest sect of the Calvinists, and could not forget my early teaching. I found too, that with this mark of Cain upon my forehead, every honourable and useful employment was barred against me; and I never met with one man in all my lifetime, until I saw my beloved Quaker friend, who showed me the least kindness, or sympathized with my mental distress, in any other way, save that of persecution, which I thought a queer way enough of manifesting the Christian spirit, and indeed, still think so. Perhaps I was unfortunate in meeting with uninformed, narrow, and bigoted men; nay, I am sure I must have been; for I have since known so many good and admirable persons, belonging to the various sects and parties, into which Christendom is, unhappily, divided, that I cannot charge Christians generally with my grievance.   Perhaps it was better that I should have thus passed through the fiery furnace alone : although I confess the flames singed me not a little.

You say this is an interesting confession to you, good Rector! and dearest brother of my heart !   Well, I knew it would be, or I should not have uttered it.   But how do you think the Quaker helped me out of my bog ?   Why, oddly enough, by trusting and loving me, and by his own great and beautiful example.   For God dwells in a good man, as in a holy temple, and cannot hide Himself there, but shews His glory in the beneficent deeds of His adopted son ; and, indeed, in endless and unspeakable ways.   And now you will be surprised when I tell you, that the revolution which he was the means of effecting in my mind, was all accomplished by silence !   From that time to this, I have never discoursed with him upon any theological question ; nor did I ever tell him what my thoughts were upon religious matters, nor what doubts and perplexities were tearing up my spirit, with their demon claws. He knew very well, however, for all that, what was going on in my thinking laboratory, and managed, by some inscrutable process, to mix gold enough amongst the base metals which were fusing in the crucible, to make a decent compound of it.

The Quaker is a man of tall stature—he will stand six feet in his shoes,—and has a head and face like Bishop Heber's; only the Bishop was a handsomer man: any portrait of the Bishop, however, if you strip him of his canonical dress, would pass for that of my friend. He is about fifty years old; his head is sprinkled over with venerable grey hairs; his eyes are overhung with thick bushy brows, and are deeply set, like dark jewels in their arches, under a noble masonry of forehead. Whilst I was living in his neighbourhood I used to walk over, in the fine summer evenings, to his hospitable hearth-side, and hold converse with him there upon all the high themes of human thought and enterprise—always excepting theology. For his mind was stored with the riches of extensive reading, and matured by age, and the experience of great and touching sorrows. So that he had always a wise word to speak upon all occasions of difficulty, as well as a large fund of knowledge, upon which he could draw to illustrate his thought, and make his arguments convincing. But you should hear him talk to form an idea of his eloquence in conversation. Behold! how his eye kindles and flashes as he warms with his subject! What rapid and startling motions he has (this quiet old Quaker), as thought after thought comes rushing down upon him for utterance. But yet withal, how solid and practical! Earnest as an old Hebrew Prophet, with a voice full of melody, and at times of unspeakable tenderness and pathos, he combines the strong sense of Cobbett, with much of the culture and power of Channing. He is the most picturesque and graphic talker I have ever listened to. He brings past scenes, persons, and events before you, as if they were present facts and occurrences. Whatever he touches rises to life by the magic of his intellect and imagination. If he had turned his attention to painting, he would have been a Claude; to poetry, he would have united in his own productions the faculties both of Rogers and Akenside. And yet he is as simple-minded as a little child. I have met with men at his table, who have come to see him from nearly all the ends of the earth: from the Borders of Lake Bikal in Buriat-Tartary, from Russia, Switzerland, and America. And what is more, he is a man worth going to see. There is no affectation about him. He works hard on his own land, and goes about very often with a white slop over his brown Quaker clothes, like a king in disguise. He has a hard, twisted, crooked hand likewise, bearing these indelible signs that a true man has used it.

In a few moments we shall be in the presence of this good friend; and now mark the house, for we are close to it. You see it is at the en-

trance of the hamlet, flanked on the right by a
semi-circle of dark trees. A long narrow garden
leads up to it; and the porch of the front door
is covered with honeysuckles and roses. On
either side the garden walk, run two flower-beds,
full of dahlias, roses, lavender, geraniums, fu-
chsias, and many rare foreign shrubs. Just beyond
these beds, on the right and left hand, are two
beautiful lawns, one of which is bounded by a
row of stately American trees. And it is a
curious fact that two of these trees (the " American ash") suffered the same kind of blight
which destroyed the potato crops in 1847; and
what is still more curious, all the ash trees in
America, with but few exceptions, shared the
same fate. Look now to the left hand, and behold that goodly range of buildings! There is
the great barn, with its white doors, where the
wheat is garnered and threshed. And see what
a host of corn, hay, and clover stacks, throngs
the yard. I can hear old "*Driver*" barking at
the pigs in the crew-yard; and yonder are all
kinds of poultry, turkeys, geese, Guinea fowl,
hens, chickens, and cock-a-doodle-do's, cackling,
quacking, and gobbling, over the "*hinderends*,"
which one of the serving girls is feeding them
with. Take care, coachman, how you drive
through the farm-yard gate. Steady. Very
good. And now, whilst the horses are getting a
feed of corn, let us go into the house.

Ah! here come all the kind and smiling faces

of the household to meet and greet us: the good wife, the fair daughter, the band of stately sons; and here, in his broad Quaker-hat, is my beloved friend himself. Well, now, suppose the welcome over; for to write down all that was said, and all the kind enquiries that were made, would be to make a dramatic instead of a descriptive and narrative paper, which I have no time to do. And seated in Thomas's best parlour, whilst the busy housewife is laying a cloth, white as snow, upon the table, and the servants are bringing in the luncheon, let us look out of the window upon the prospect before us. The sun is high up in heaven; and the light of his glory lies all over the landscape, which stretches away in one great level plain, dotted with farms, and made picturesque with waving corn-fields and trees. The high Cliffe-road shuts in the landscape.

Many a time, in years that are gone by, have I sat at this open window, watching the changing scenery of the clouds, and the wonderful effect of light and shadow on the green landscape below. I wish I could paint all that I see and feel, at such times; but Nature is like a fairy, —she vanishes the moment you come too near her; and will not have her secrets made known to vulgar ears. Or, more properly speaking, she is a beautiful coquette, who tosses her head at admirers, and though often wooed, is never won.

But come, set to ; for the luncheon is ready.
And talking of luncheon reminds me of tea.
You have no idea what a tea is in this house.
There are ham and beef, doe-nuts and hot Lin-
colnshire-cakes, and bread, white and brown,—
with plates full of rich butter, hard by. And
there are clotted-cream too, and sweet spice-
cakes, and preserves, and apple and mince pies,
made upon large plates, after the American
fashion—for my friend lived twenty-six years in
America, and all his children are American born
—a tea, evidently fit for none other than honest
men, as good old Izaak Walton would say.
And that we may all partake of it with thankful,
joyous hearts (for I am speaking as if it were
tea-time, and remembering with pleasure many
such times), let us be silent, whilst our true
friend and host, reads awhile from the Family
Bible.

He opens the sacred pages at the Book of
Ruth, perhaps ;—for he knows where the Bible-
poetry lies, and loves its Bucolics, better I think,
than its Tragedies.—Strong-hearted, affectionate
Ruth ! how I have loved thee, and Nature, and
the East, with its golden corn-fields, ever since
I heard thy story from the lips of my friend.
And now come the pause, and the silent prayer;
after which the bell rings, and the rosy servant
girls bring in the tea-urn, " hissing hot, like a
horse-shoe," as Falstaff says, and smoking away
with a real gusto, as if it enjoyed the fun.

Good as the tea was, however, on such occasions, the Host's conversation was better. He knew all the American policy, and was well acquainted with its manœuvres. He could tell you tales about Daniel Webster, his early history, his speeches, and public career. He had a great fund of historical anecdotes (and has yet; for hark what a long yarn he is at this moment spinning to his listening guests, about the "Niggers," and "Chesapeake Bay," during the time of the revolutionary war). He can give you more sketches of Yankee character, than Sam Slick saw in all his wanderings. He was one of the little band of heroes, that stood out in Massachusetts against the iniquitous system of slavery in America; and with Loyd Garrison, Arthur Tappan, and others, projected the Anti-Slavery Society. It was in his house at Salem, that George Thompson, M. P., was mobbed; and it was he who saved Thompson's life on that occasion. I very well remember with what stirring interest he told me all the particulars of that fearful riot. Thompson was to have lectured that night in Salem; but the friends of the Anti-Slavery Society found that men from Boston, and planters from the Southern States, were assembling in motley groups in the Market-place, and near the Lycæum. They heard it whispered also that a conspiracy was formed for carrying Thompson off to Boston, where he was to be publicly " tarred and fea-

thered," and in all probability murdered.   Nay,
one of the fleetest horses in the State had been
hired for this purpose, and all the toll-bars between Salem and Boston were paid, and ordered
to be left open, that no impediment might stop
them on the way, when they had once seized
their victim.   The Anti-Slavery friends, however, prevented Thompson from lecturing; and
when the mob found he did not come at the
appointed time, they grew mad and furious.   It
was well known that Thompson had been stay-
ing, for some weeks, at our friend's house, and
the cry was raised to mob him there.   Now the
house was situated a quarter of a mile out of
Salem; and thanks to the fleet foot of a friend,
these tidings were borne thither long before the
mob arrived.   Thompson was immediately conveyed to a neighbouring wood, with injunctions
to lie close there, and abide the issue.   In the
meanwhile, our friend Thomas, with the aid
of two or three stout neighbours, barred all
his doors, barricaded his windows, and silently
awaited the arrival of the mob.   At last they
came, shouting, hallooing, yelling, and uttering
all manner of oaths, and horrible blasphemies.
A strong rail fenced the front garden; and the
rioters stopped there, whilst half a dozen of the
ringleaders leapt over it, and thundered at the
house door.   There were lights in all the bed-
room windows; and in one room in the second
story, on the left hand, the blinds were drawn

up, and the brave wife of our friend was walking to and fro, with her newly-born infant in her arms. The knocking at the door continued, and the mob were growing more and more furious. At last Thomas threw up the window over the porch, and demanded the meaning of this outrage upon a peaceable citizen.

"We want Thompson—Turn out Thompson!" said they.

Thomas replied that Thompson was not in the house.

"But I saw him in that top room to-day," cried a voice from the mob.

"That may, or may not be true," was the quiet reply. "And what I now say is, that he is not here, and if he were, I would not give him up to you."

"Then let us have the Quaker!" cried a ruffianly fellow below. But he was immediately silenced by a powerful, gigantic man, who came forward and said :—

"If Thompson ain't in your place, Quaker! no man here shall hurt you."

"I give you my word again," was the reply, "that he is not here."

"Where is he then? Tell us that; or we'll burn your house over your head !" cried another ruffian.

"He left my house to-day; and I shall not tell you where he went, even though you carry your threat into execution, and burn me and my little ones together."   And with that, the brave Quaker shut down the window.

"I guess they'll smash in the winders and doors jist now," said a rough Yankee neighbour, as Thomas turned to speak to him: "so I vote," he continued, "that we go down stairs, and look arter 'um."

"They will do what they are permitted to do," said our friend, "and no more."

"That's very true," answered the Yankee, "and I'll take care they ain't permitted to come in here, without a broken head or two, and no mistake!"   So he took up a poker from the kitchen fire-place, and after examining it in a a very cool and business-like way, pronounced it "the very weepon, to teach the critters manners."

Fortunately, there was no necessity for this poker discipline; for just as the mob were arranging their tar and flax, to set fire to the house, a strong band of magistrates, clergymen, gentry, and merchants, came riding up to the house, from Salem; and by their vigorous efforts and firmness the mob was dispersed.

Thompson, after spending so many horrible hours, in the wild jungle of the forest, was hunted up by his friends (who would have found him much sooner than they did, only he mistook them for his enemies, and retreated silently as they advanced).   He was conveyed away in the morning to a farm-house, about

LEAVES FROM SHERWOOD FOREST.

twelve miles off, and was nearly discovered on the road. However, he arrived at his hiding-place safely; and waited there until a ship from Boston was ready to sail for England. And at the last moment, when the vessel was getting under weigh, Thompson arrived at the dock, in a cab, jumped on board, and was soon clear of the " Land of Liberty !"

For fear lest the cab-driver should have re-cognised Thompson, he was ordered to drive out of town directly, to some place about four miles off. For if he had recognised him, and given out the news in Boston, the Lynch-boys would have been after him in boats, or followed him with a steamer until they had caught him, and brought him back. He was obliged to leave his wife and children behind him at our friend's house, and they did not return to England until some weeks after he had sailed.

Well, now that I have done gossipping, and related all my incongruous episodes, let us start, if you please, dear friends, for Sherwood. Come, Thomas, harness the grey horse—Longshanks I mean—the same fellow that brought you and John Kendall to see me at T——d; and take Emma with you; she will made us all merry with her tales and laughter; and a fine time we shall have of it, in the old Forest, this bright day. Come, no excuses; we are here on purpose to carry you off. A glass of wine with you, good Rector, if you please; and here's to our friends,

present and absent. Now then, ladies, let us
depart in peace ; and so, good bye, and God's
best blessings rest upon all you who remain behind,—and, indeed, upon us who go ; for why
not ?

Gentle (surly, fastidious, or indifferent, it's
all one to me, only I will call you gentle out of
courtesy)—Gentle reader, then, imagine us, if
you please, at Edwinstowe, the capital of Sherwood Forest, and prepare yourself for fresh
company.

We arrived at this pretty little village, about
one o'clock ; passing through Saxelby, over the
iron bridge at Dunham (which crosses the river
Trent, and is so lofty, that the vessels can pass
under it in full sail) ; through Great Markham,
Tuxford, and Ollerton.

Ollerton is about two miles from Edwinstowe,
and the most interesting part of the Forest.—
Bilhaugh commences just beyond the meadows,
a little to the right of the town, as you journey
towards Edwinstowe. A fine trout-stream sepa-
rates Ollerton from the Forest ; and a sweet,
musical voice it has, I assure you. I am fond
of listening to streams and rivers, and remember
many snatches of the songs they sing. But the
Wharfe is my divinest minstrel ; as you will
discover, if you should ever read a little book I
have edited, called " *Sketches of Country
Scenery.*" But it is time I should introduce you
to the good people of Edwinstowe, who accom-

panied us to the Forest on this memorable day.
I ought to tell you that they were old friends of
mine, and that we had passed many a pleasant
hour together in the "old Wood," as they call
it, long before this occasion. Well, we—that is
to say, the Rector, and the ladies of his household, the Quaker, and his pretty, merry daughter, and myself—went first of all to Christopher
Thompson's cottage, at the top of the village.

We found him at work in his garden, and
directly he saw us enter the gate, he dashed his
spade into the ground, and came forward with
his hearty right hand, to welcome us. He is a
man of middle age—somewhere between forty
and sixty; for it is difficult to tell his age by
his looks, he is so hale and strong. He has a
fine face, which would look well in a picture.—
His cheeks are stained with the fire of the morning; his eyes are bright and intelligent; his
hair long, and streams over his shoulders, like
the white locks of one of Ossian's storm-heroes.
He is English to the back-bone, and has done
and suffered much in his time. Less than
twenty years ago he was a wandering player,
and painter-general to the theatrical establishment. He fell in love with Edwinstowe, however, and resolved to settle there as a house and
decorative painter. In a few years he changed
the face of his adopted village, by opening evening classes, gratis, to all the villagers, and by
establishing an artizan's library and lecture-

room. Civilization sprung up under his wise
rule, and now he enjoys the fruits of his labours,
and looks with pleasure upon the intelligence
and good morals of the people around him.   He
is a landscape painter, too, and his pictures of
forest scenery are as truthful as Nature herself.
We found the walls of his parlour covered all
over with the works of his easel; in little
niches, on each side the fire-place, were busts of
the poets, placed over goodly rows of books.—
He is married, and has twelve or thirteen children—a whole house full at least—although I
am not sure about the exact number.   There is a
poet in the family, and I cannot say how many
singers and musicians.

We invited burly Christopher to spend the
day with us in the Forest; and in a short time
we hunted up John Trueman, and Robert
Widdison—the former, a first-rate entymologist,
who, although a shoemaker by trade, corresponds
with the first men and societies in the kingdom,
and is known as a valuable entymological con-
tributor to the cabinets of our national institutions; the latter a sculptor, musician, and
musical composer.   In a short time, therefore,
we were all seated under the branches of the
"*Major Oak,*" about which something will be
said by and by.   A white cloth was spread
over the green sward, and upon this were
placed the provisions, which were to constitute
our forest-banquet.   Our friend, the Rector,

officiated as butler, and was not sparing of his Champagne, which did not grieve me, because it made the ladies merry. Beside, I knew that the Burgundy would make its appearance before long, and I meant to do justice to it. The Quaker—to his honour be it spoken —did not refuse a solitary glass of wine which the Honourable Miss M. presented to him with her own fair hand—how indeed could he? I would have drank aquafortis if she had offered it to me. Our Quaker, however, is a very abstemious man, and rarely drinks anything but water; and his little favourite, pet girl, is a teetotaller, God bless her! Not so Christopher, Trueman, Widdison, and Company; for we all enjoyed ourselves very much, and poured out, I know not how many libations, to Pan and the wood-gods.

When we had finished eating and drinking, our lady friend, the "Princess," who was always for mixing intellectual pleasures with those of the senses, inquired who were the poets and authors that had written about Sherwood; and Christopher (who loves the Forest and every body that has set forth its praises) pulled three or four books from the ample pockets of his coat, and began to tell over the names of these literary persons, in answer to the lovely Princess.

"I have here, a few volumes," he said, "in which you will find various descriptive accounts

E

of Sherwood, by men who are its enthusiastic
admirers. I always come prepared, on occasions
like this; and the books, sweet lady, are at
your disposal."

"We hardly need books," said the Quaker,
"to help us to admire this lovely scenery,
although I for one, shall be glad to listen to any
thing which may be read about it. Look at
those fine oaks and sunny glades before us, how
beautiful they are! And those glorious ferns,
and patches of yellow gorse and purple heather,
how finely they set off the dark greenery of the
trees. And then on the other side of the glade,
opposite this noble oak, do but see what a fairy-
land of birches wave their long musical locks,
and fair white arms, in the golden sunlight!
Books cannot paint like Nature."

"True," said the Rector; "but who would
have thought to hear so amorous and poetical a
description from the owner of thy drab coat,
friend Thomas? I propose that the 'Princess'
read us an account of Sherwood, to balance your
enthusiasm; for written books can bear no comparison with impulsive speech, which comes out
of the depths of a heart like yours. So may it
please your Majesty, read!"

"Ah!" said we all, "Read! Read! 'an it
please your Majesty." Whereupon the "Princess" wrapped herself up in the Rector's plaid,
and leaning back against the Old Oak, who
trembled when he felt the beautiful burden,

against his old rough heart, read as follows, from a little volume, entitled " *Walks round Huddersfield.*"

ROBIN HOOD'S GRAVE.

We are going to visit the Grave of Robin Hood, whose name is a household word amongst us, and whose memory is a national possession. For nearly 600 years he has rested in Kirklees Park, amongst our venerable hills. The Calder rolls below him, through the same quiet and beautiful valley which it made glad with its presence when the true-hearted outlaw went down into the eternal silences. The same heavens are above him ; the same earth is under him ; but otherwise all is changed. The nunnery wherein he was well nigh bled to death, in order to satisfy the enmity of Roger of Doncaster, is clean gone ; vanished like a dream for ever, with all its nuns and appurtenances. Roger and the Prioress are likewise gone, and have their doom. Two old relics of that past time only remain, and these are the lodge-chamber in which Robin died, and the old hostel of the nunnery. Robin lies all alone there, with the exception of these. Little John, the Naylor, sleeps at Hathersedge, amongst the blue limestone rocks of Derbyshire ; and all the merry men, with their Lincoln green coats and gold adornments, their archery and bugle horns, are scattered also, and lie in unknown graves, until the louder bugle of the resurrection shall awake and reunite them. All is changed. We have had our Henry the Eighth since then; our Protestantism, and Commonwealth; our manufactures, commerce, steam engines, and electric telegraphs; our free press, so called, and our Protestant philosophies and literature. And at the very foot of Robin Hood's grave, fifty trains a-day thunder along between the two towns of Leeds and Manchester. Fancy the sudden awaking of good old Robin into this world of the nineteenth century. Fancy him unurned, standing upon the edge of that high terrace of rocks which overlooks the vale of Calder. Yonder goes a railway train with its horse of fire, thundering along the iron road; and there stands Robin, with his green tunic, his bugle, his bow and arrows, wondering what it all means.

It will be necessary, however, before we go a step on this proposed walk of ours, that I should speak more definitely about Robin Hood, and say something about his birthplace and history. And as it is lawful for a writer to quote from himself, especially when he cannot say better in new words what he has already said in old ones, I will make certain extracts here from an article written by me on "Sherwood Forest," in the June No. of the *People's Journal* for 1848, which will supply all the information necessary for our purpose.

"So many conflicting statements have been made respecting this noble outlaw (Robin Hood) that he was fast becoming a myth, until Spencer Hall, 'The Sherwood Forester,' rescued him about six years ago,* from the embranglements and defacements of time, and restored him to us in as good flesh and blood as we could expect under the circumstances. We learn from various sources, that Robin Hood was born at Loxley Chase, near Sheffield, in the beginning of the thirteenth century; and I fully agree with Spencer Hall, after an examination of all the documents upon the subject which have fallen in my way, that Robin was no more Earl of Huntingdon than he was Seneschal of France. The most ancient traditions, as well as the most authenticated ballads, agree in describing him as a *yeoman*, driven to the woods by his hatred of the oppression of his time. *The Lytell Geste of Robyn Hode*, very plainly calls Robin a ' Yeoman;' and as the *Geste* itself bears, in its entire structure, grouping, and keen discrimination of character, the genius of our venerable Chaucer, there can be little question of the fidelity of the appellation. The accounts of Robin's appearance and accoutrements, which we find in the ballads of Editor Ritson, are still further corroborations of our hero's rank; and I have no doubt, as Chaucer's men and women are all *types*

* In a book which he called " The Forester's Offering."

E 3

of *classes*, that Robin Hood is literally described in the Yeoman of the Canterbury Pilgrims.

" 'Little can be known,' says Spencer Hall, 'of our hero's progress up to the time when the patriots arose, under Simon de Montfort, Earl of Leicester, to enforce the recognition of *Magna Charta*, by Henry III.; but that his powers were devoted to the side of his country's rights in that memorable movement, &c., there can be no doubt.' Fordun, a noteworthy chronicler, who lived about a century after this movement, says, in the *Scotichronicon*, 'after relating the final defeat of the great national party, consequent on the battle of Evesham, in August, 1265, that from among the dispossessed and banished arose Robin Hood and Little John, with their accomplices, whom the people of his time were extravagantly fond of celebrating in tragedy and comedy beyond all others.' It was only in later times, to 'give a tawdry effect to ill-written plays,' that Robin Hood was styled Earl of Huntingdon. To the general manly and noble character of this bold outlaw, who believed in more '*points*' than were ever contained in any English '*Charter*,' we have the most unequivocal testimony in history and the popular traditions. He seems to me, as I read of him surrounded by his little court of outlaws, in the old Forest of Sherwood, like an aboriginal lord of Nature's own fashioning and appointment. There is such a large free heart in him, and so wise a head upon his shoulders, that I cannot wonder how the 'disaffected' came to him in those troublesome times, and listed themselves to his generous service. In his rule and person was exhibited the very singular governmental riddle of *despotic democracy*. This Rob o'th'Wood was the strongest man of all the strong men who owned him Liege and Master. His strength lay in his brains and heart, however, not in his bones and fibres; although he understood, no doubt, all the tricks of wrestling, cuffing, and quarter-staff. It was a fine sight, I will answer for it, to see him and his true men, in their liveries of gold and green, symbolical of the forest garniture, and adapted, moreover, to deceive sheriff's and king's officers, who might be on the look out for them over the landscape. Just fancy a hundred of such men, attired in this manner, with their bows and staves, drawn up in review before Robin Hood, previous to an excursion against some company of priests and their vassals, who are returning from the distraint of a poor yeoman over the copses of Barnsdale. There is Little John, the Naylor, seven feet high, with a droll red face, cracking sundry jests with Much, the miller's son; who, on another occasion, according to the *Lytell Geste*, asked with sinister meaning, when Robin Hood was endowing the poor Knight—whether the '*money was well told!*' And there, too, is Scathelock, who assured Much, on the same occasion, with a good horse laugh, when Little John was measuring out the 'cloth' with his 'bowe tree,' that John might give the knight— 'better measure, for—

'By —— it cost him but lite.'

And these good fellows, with Will Stutely (Stoutly) and old Friar Tuck, as the captains of the little band, each ready to go where he is sent, and that right merrily too, and without grumbling; whether to chase a sheriff, or way-lay an abbot.

"I must not omit to mention, however, that Robin Hood was addicted to two things, which, as I believe, are common to all noble natures, viz., love and music. He had his harper, in the person of Allan o' the Dale, 'a very gentle character,' as Spencer Hall says, 'whose mind is said to have been injured by a cross in his affections;' and he found his love in the beautiful Maid Marian. It must not be supposed from this attachment, that Robin was a free-booter amongst women; for no fact is better attested concerning him, than that he had a respect, amounting even to reverence, for the fair sex, and was always their friend and defender. The ballad which relates the circumstance of his death, from which I shall perhaps quote more largely by and by, has these lines :—

'I never hurt woman in all my life,
Nor man in woman's companie.'

Besides which, in deference to the ecclesiastical law of our time, I will even venture to hint, that old Friar Tuck—who was a 'better,' and no doubt a 'sadder' man, than the novelists have made him—might have married them in the moonlight, under the green-wood tree, whilst gentle Allen made rich extemporaneous music, such as the brooks and breezes sing, out of the chords of his much-loved instrument.

"However this may be, I am quite sure that no one could join Simon de Montfort, and being defeated, return to the fastnesses of the Forest, rather than give up his liberty, with a priest, a musician, and a Maid Marian for consort, and be a bad man. These four things are impossible to a bad man.

"Besides which, we hear instances of Robin's devotion and reverence for religion, which really invest him with a true moral grandeur. The writer of an article in the ' *Westminster Review*,' No. 65, quoted by Mr. Hall in his ' *Life of Robin Hood*,' has given us the following translation of an old Latin chronicler upon this subject : ' Once upon a time, in Barnesdale, when he was avoiding the wrath of the king and the rage of the prince, while engaged in very devoutly hearing mass, *as he was wont to do*, nor would he interrupt the service for any occasion ; one day, I say, whilst so at mass, it happened that a certain viscount, and other officers of the king, who had often before molested him, were seeking after him in that retired woodland spot wherein he was thus occupied. Those of his men who first discovered this pursuit, came and entreated him to fly with all speed; but this, from reverence for the consecrated host, which he was then most devoutly adoring, he absolutely refused to do. Whilst the rest of the people were trembling for fear of death, Robert alone confiding in him whom he fearlessly worshipped, with the very few whom he had then beside him, encountered his enemies, overcame them with ease, was enriched by their spoils, and was thus induced to hold ministers of the church and masses (only the good ministers though; for he loved to fleece none so much as a bad priest!) in greater veneration than ever, as mindful of the common saying :—" God hears the man that often hears the mass." '

" There are various other traditions concerning Robin Hood, which, whether true or false, are valuable, as evidences of the general impress which his character and actions stamped upon the memory of his time. Noble, generous, and brave—a lover of the poor, and defender of their rights against the rich and the oppressor, he comes down to us like the hero of some old dim epic, whose author has taxed all the powers of his imagination to set in the most costly jewels of humanity. His encounter with Edward the First, for instance, is full of human beauty.— This king had offered large rewards for Robin, alive or dead, but none of his officers and spies could find him out. So having conquered the Welsh, he came down to Sherwood, resolved to try what he could do with his blood-hounds and most trusty followers, in the way of extirpating the outlaw and his merry men. It is said that he took up his abode at Clipston Castle, and scoured the whole country round for many days without success. At last he went in disguise, and wandered about the Forest alone, in hope of meeting with his enemies. All these things were well known to Robin Hood, who managed to have *his* spies at Clipston Castle. It was not long, therefore, before Robin showed himself to the king, in full array of green and gold, equipped also with his bow and arrows, his short sword, and that little bugle-horn about which Edward had heard so many magical stories.— The king demanded who this apparition of the woods might be?

" ' I am Robin Hood,' answered the outlaw, nothing daunted at the presence of majesty.

" ' Then,' returned the king, 'we are well met, so stand upon your guard.'

" But Robin wound his horn, and a hundred armed men rose up from the gorse and heather, as if by enchantment, demanding the will of their leader. ' It is to do reverence to the King of England that I have called you,' said he; and Edward was so touched with this generous spectacle, that he invited Robin and his men to court, with a promise of free pardon and protection. It is further said, that the invitation was accepted, and that the Maid Marian died during the year that Robin was at court. He was deeply affected at the loss of his beloved; and when spring returned, he was so haunted with the olden memories of the woods, their sweet liberty, flowers, brooks, and birds, that he left the king by permission, and returned to his old haunts and companions. So, at all events, runs the tradition.

" I cannot leave Robin without adding a few words upon his death and burial-place. Within four miles of the spot where I am now writing, there was, in those olden times, a religious house called the NUNNERY OF KIRKLEES, at the head of which Robin's cousin was appointed in the capacity of prioress. In his eightieth year, the outlaw, still strong in heart and limb, was journeying that way, and was taken suddenly ill.—— In his extremity he applied for aid at the nunnery; and tradition says that, in order to please Sir Roger de Doncaster, who was a great man in the neighbourhood in those days, she caused him to be bled well nigh unto death. When Little John heard these sad tidings—for it was soon known to the dependents of the nunnery, and the brave old Naylor, who was never far away from his master—he forced his way into the chamber of the dying hero, and besought him to authorise the calling together of the band, for the purpose of burning 'Kirkley Hall, and all their nunnery,' as the old ballad has it.   But the noble outlaw felt that he was closing his earthly account, and had no wish to draw any further upon Heaven's justice or forgiveness; so he answered Little John in these words—

> " ' I never hurt fair maid in all my time,
>   Nor at my end shall it be ;
>   But take my bent bow in thy hand,
>   And a broad arrow let thou flee ;
>   And where this arrow is taken up,
>   There shall my grave digged be.
>
> " ' Lay me a green sod under my head,
>   And another at my feet ;
>   And lay my bent bow by my side,
>   Which was my music sweet ;
>   And make my grave of gravel and green,
>   Which is most right and meet.'

And there, in the beautiful park of Kirklees, sleep the ashes of this venerable patriot.   The park is situated upon a high platform, close to Cooper Bridge Station, on the Manchester and Leeds Railway, which commands a magnificent sweep of country, including the fine old hills of Huddersfield, the romantic vale of Calder, and the far off, interminable moors, which run with but little intervals, along the 'Backbone' mountains of England, right into North Britain. The grave of Robin Hood is fenced round with iron palisades, set with solid stone masonry, and covered with a large slab, and brought, most likely, from

F

the grave-yard of the Nunnery. The head-stone contains an inscription, setting forth the valour, generosity, and woodland gifts of the dead. The old Abbey Lodge still stands; and the room in which Robin died, and the window from which the arrow was shot, are still shown to the pilgrim who goes up thither. A part of the ancient hostel of the Abbey is likewise in existence, and retains its former usage; for it is a public house of entertainment for man and beast, and is well known by the sign of 'The Three Nuns.'"

I have said now what seemed to me necessary, about the history and death of the English Out-law. Who will go up with me, then, to see the grave where he lies? We shall have a pleasant walk of it, especially by the route I mean to take you; which is, you will soon discover, through all manner of high-ways and bye-ways. Let us set out, then, upon the Bradford Road, and whilst you, my companion, are enjoying the beautiful scenery by the way, I will talk to you about Sherwood Forest, which was the wild woodland home of the dead Outlaw for so many years. I know that old Forest all by heart, and have its varied scenes stored like pictures in my memory. It is much changed now from what it was when Robin Hood dwelt in it; but it is still very extensive, and many of its olden features are preserved.

You pass through it on the high road between

Newark and Worksop; and just beyond Ollerton you get a glimpse of its character from the grey, gnarled, and knotted oaks, which guard the forest on either side. But it would be impossible to conceive from this slight view how strange, wild, and wonderful are the revelations of beauty and sublimity which unfold themselves in the primeval sanctuary of the Forest itself. Hundreds of travellers pass that way, without ever suspecting they are on the borders of an enchanted world. And yet the walk of a quarter of a mile from that well-paved macadamised road will conduct you to an old realm of trees, with huge barkless trunks and twisted branches, which look like the giant skeletons of an extinct creation. There is a solitude around them, likewise, which fills the heart with new, startling, and painful emotions. This part of the Forest is called Bilhaugh, and stretches eastward away for two or three miles. The trees are all oaks—some of them eighty feet in height—bare and black; scarred by the storm and riven by the lightning. Many of them are split in twain from the top to the bottom; and yet so strong is the old life within them, that their branches are covered with foliage. Imagine these old forest patriarchs, alive with God ten hundred years ago, putting on new garments of green every Spring to hide the nakedness of age, and daily dying a death which it will take centuries yet to consummate. It is the most affecting sight which a man can behold, to witness these huge, dumb creatures—so silent, and yet so desolate.

Few persons, unaccustomed to observe Nature in her ancient hiding-places, would credit the singular transformations which the oaks of Bilhaugh have, in many instances, undergone. It would be quite possible to make a new heraldry from the strange emblematic devices which have been carved upon them by the invisible fingers of the elements. Dragons, crocodiles' heads, serpents, glaring basilisks, kraken, and monsters of an unknown birth, surmount the capitols of the old trees, or grin under their barkless ribs. You are literally shut out, in this part of the Forest, from all signs of civilization, and seem to stand in a " strange, solemn, and old universe." Over you hang the azure vaults of immensity; and under your feet how many worlds lie buried !

> " Heaven silent above us,
> Graves under us silent."

The decayed ferns in some places form a soil which is yards in depth, and the surface is covered with mosses in beautiful variety, and studded with bluebells, violets, foxgloves, and other sweet wild flowers, in their appointed seasons. In the Spring, whilst the ferns lie dead and yellow around you, and the oaks are blanched and leafless, the solitude is broken by rooks and jackdaws building their nests in the hollow sockets of the trees, and waving their dusky pennons to the music of their own cawing; or if some tiny bird flits through the colossal ruins of the Forest, it is only to utter mournful threnes, or sad melancholy pipings. The rooks and daws are the only winged creatures (save the night owls) which have any claim of habitancy in this old primeval temple. But as the warm days come on, and May returns to earth, like a bride laden with flowers, there is an universal joyousness in the old Forest; the mighty oaks, with centuries in their blood, leap up as into life eternal, and clap their ancient hands with a great shout of deliverance and praise. The gorse, dropping with gold and delicious odours, flourishes under the wide foliage of the trees; the fiery adders come from their Winter holes and sun themselves in the glades, and the whole Forest resounds with the melody of birds. At night, when the shadows cast by the moon enhance the solemnity of the scene, and fill it with ghostly witcheries and wonderful enchantments, you may hear the love-lorn song of the nightingale, rushing through the starry air from the far off dells of Birkland, and dying away in sweet cadences as they are borne along from echo to echo. The hares and rabbits then come out of the dingles and thick entangled underwood, to crop the dewy herbage, and gambol in the silence and

security of the hour; and as you walk along,
the startled pheasant rushes to the tree tops
with heavy wing and shrill cries.

But I would advise those who can afford the
time and the money, to run down from Huddersfield by rail to Eckington station, and walk
thence to Edwinstowe, the capital of Sherwood,
and visit the old Forest themselves. I can
assure them they will be amply repaid, both in
body and mind, for the excursion. Bilhaugh
alone, is worth travelling a hundred miles bare-
foot to see, and once seen it can never be forgotten. Pemberton, the "Wanderer," as he
called himself, walked from London to spend
one day there, and then returned, grateful that
he was strong enough to make so beautiful a
pilgrimage. Washington Irving, Elliott, Howitt,
and numberless other men, known and unknown
to fame, have spent many days in this venerable wilderness, which extends even now, in all
its olden features, eight or ten miles in length,
by two or three in breadth. And the reader
must not suppose that this is any ordinary
region; or that he can see the like of it in
Epping, or in any of the other ancient forests. I
have been in the back woods of the American
continent, and have seen many noble " green
robed senators" of the forest in England, but I
never knew what a tree was until I beheld the
giants of Sherwood. I will describe some of
them more particularly by and bye; and in the

meanwhile let me allude to the historical associations which belong to them. In the first place, they connect us with the descendants of *Hu* the Mighty—with the Druid life and Bardic Institutions of Britain—anterior even to the Roman invasion. For there is no question that Sherwood is a part of the aboriginal forests of the island. Its antiquity may be gathered from the fact that there are still the remains of Roman roads, villas, and encampments in various parts of it. Long, therefore, before the organisation of the Saxon Heptarchy, the trees of Sherwood were in the full vigour of youth and glory. And afterwards, the old kings of Mercia hunted the wolf and the wild boar in its shaggy dens and brakes. In the time of William the Conqueror, various Norman barons held it under the tenure of service to the Crown ; and many cruel forest laws—out of which our modern game laws grew—were enacted to preserve the red deer from the " *short buts and long buts*" of the conquered Saxon peasantry. He who kills a buck shall have his eyes put out ; he who steals a doe shall be hanged. These are specimens of those feudal laws ; and, I am sorry to say, the spirit of them is not much improved in our game laws. If any woodman, lingcropper, villager, or traveller, of this day, were to kill a hare, pheasant, or even a rabbit, in the forest, he would be liable to a fine of eighty pounds, and in default of payment must go into the county jail as a prisoner during the Queen's pleasure; which is often of very long duration. There are men now in Nottingham jail who have been imprisoned there for five years under the very circumstances I have named. John Bright will, perhaps, set them at liberty before long; and no one will thank him more heartily than myself.

In the time of King John, the hays of Birkland—of which I shall speak more particularly by and bye—and the woods of Bilhaugh were the scenes of many royal hunting excursions; for John loved the chase quite as much as he hated liberty; and was a frequent guest at the old castle of Clipstone, which then stood proudly on a hill about a mile and a half from Edwinstowe. Now, however, even the name of the owner of the castle is forgotten, and nothing but a heap of ruins is left to indicate the site of that feudal hold. A few pretty cottages with neat gardens, occupied by the retainers of the present Duke of Portland, lie scattered at the foot of the hill, and constitute the village of Clipstone. The scenery all round it is very romantic and beautiful, and one of the best trout streams in England meanders through it, which, however, no man may fish, unless he wishes to be *caught*.

I should like to speak about the Cresswell Crags and Markland Grips, which are close to Welbeck, the residence of the Duke of Portland, and are still pointed out by the peasantry as

Robin's Winter quarters. The *River Wollen* runs far below their summits into the lake at Welbeck, and there are subterranean caverns in the Crags, which are called Robin Hood's chamber, pantry, and parlour. But I have no time to dwell upon these matters, for we are already close to Mr. Firth's mansion, and I wish to occupy the remaining part of the time it will take us to walk to Brighouse, in giving you some idea of the size of the oaks of Sherwood, and of the glorious hays of Birkland.

The " *Major Oak* " is of almost incredible dimensions. When you stand in front of it, it looks like a huge castle; and although eleven persons can pack themselves inside it, the old wooden walls are not half worn out. Spencer Hall, about four years ago, led me blindfolded to this tree, and made me feel it inside and out, before I took the bandage from my eyes. The illusion was wonderful. I could not, until I saw it with both eyes, believe that it was one concrete substance of a tree that I was handling. At 6 inches from the ground its trunk is 90 feet in circumference, at 6 feet from the ground, 30 feet in circumference; circumference of one of the arms, at a distance of 4 feet from the trunk, 12 feet; circumference at the extent of its branches, 140 feet; interior of the trunk, 20 feet in circumference, and 15 feet in height.— Altogether, and every inch of it, what I call a *tree*.

F 3

A few yards from this majestic oak, you cross the broad woodland glade, called Cockglade, because game-cocks were once kept in the Major Oak, which divides the hays of Birkland from Bilhaugh. And here a new world of wonder and beauty bursts upon you. As far as the eye can reach, over upland and valley, there is a magnificent array of birches, with their graceful silvery trunks and waving foliage, through which the breezes, when they are soft and low, make musical dirges, like the sound of a far-off sea.

There could not be a more startling and picturesque contrast than the birches of Birkland and the oaks of Bilhaugh. Caliban and Miranda are here married together according to God's oldest ceremonies. As you pass up this broad glade or riding, you are often arrested by the grotesque forms of the oaks; and not unfrequently a troop of young birches are seen waving their fair arms and tresses over one of these solitaries, who, grim and sullen, appears as if he had been caught out of bounds, and were suddenly enchanted by these beautiful nymphs. Beautiful they are, indeed! for they have attained a stature and maturity which I never saw in any similar trees.

I should like to describe the ruined "*Shambles Oak*" to you, and the fine larch and heather scenery in the neighbourhood of it, and the vast forest of white thorn, which, in the month of

May, when it is in full blossom and the sun
shines on it, looks like a burning sea of snow ;
but we are close to Brighouse now, and I. can
only speak of the " great glade" of Sherwood,
which the Duke of Portland has cut and railed
for eight miles through the forest, and planted
with avenues of the dark green cedars of Le-
banon. At the extremity of this magnificent
riding, near Clipstone, the good Duke has erected
a splendid *lodge*, which, in its architectural design, is a copy, as I have heard, of a certain
monastic gateway at Worksop. It is used as a
central school-house, although it is half a mile
from any other dwelling, for the children who
live in the scattered hamlets of the forest. On
the north side, if I remember rightly, there are
effigies of King Richard the Lion-hearted, Allan
o' Dale, and Friar Tuck ; on the south side there
are similar sculptures of Robin Hood, Little
John, and Maid Marian.

But here we are on the bridge, under which
the Leeds and Manchester railway runs, leading
to Brighouse. The "Railway Hotel," and the
Brighouse station, are on the right of us, and
that road to the left leads up to Raistrick, where
my old and much-loved friends, the Quakers,
have founded a noble school. Brighouse is a
manufacturing village, as you may see by the
tall chimnies, and the troops of factory children
playing at shuttlecock in the streets. We have
very little to do, however, with Brighouse ; so

let us pass through it, and turn away upon the
Clifton road, in the direction of Leeds; for
Kirklees Park lies up that way. This wood by
the roadside, covering the hills on our left, is
called Clifton Wood; and as I am pretty well
known now for a trespasser, it will require no
apology, on my part, for the *fresh* trespass which
must here be perpetrated. So let us climb over
the stone wall, and enter the wood.

Here we are knee-deep in blue bells, which in
this month of May literally cover the whole side
of the hills like a garment of azure; and look
you! we have startled a little bird from the
brown grass at our feet, and here is its nest. See
what rich, beautiful eggs are there! And behold how the tiny warbler perches itself on the
spray of yonder hazel, and with sad musical
utterances seems to beseech us not to disturb its
little home. Ah, no! thou piping denizen of the
wild woods! God has given thee a home—and
I, indeed, will not injure either it or thee.

The wood is full of young, graceful trees;
the ash, hazel, oak, and flowering alder, are all
here. But if you would command the vale of
Calder, you must mount higher, up to the very
top of the hill. You will find a path there,
close to the hawthorn hedge which divides the
wood from the pastures on the other side. If
you look through the hedge, you will see another
wood over the pastures, arrayed in glorious
brown and green foliage. Houses dot the wood-

side, and there are many little children playing before them and around them. Right over the valley rise other hills, clad in the richest verdure, which face us with a kingly majesty. We have a full view of Brighouse, with its smoky chimnies, also on the right; and at the foot of the hills, on the other side of the valley, the white iron rails of the steam-road gleam in the sunshine, like the trail of a fiery serpent.

What a still, calm day it is! As you walk along through the shady avenues of the trees, you can hear the roar of steam-engines, and the thunder and hammering in the Brighouse foundries. Almost every step you take, discovers new beauties in the vast expanse of landscape which lies in and beyond the vale of Calder. Here, through a vista in the trees, you look down upon a quiet pastoral country, with the sheep lying in the sun, and scattered oxen grazing amongst them. All else is shut out from sight; there is no sign of manufactures, or of any modern enterprise. Our old friend Pan, rules there; and you might fancy the music of that rill which comes up to us from below, was the sound of his oaten-pipe. And then, as you advance a little further, the scene changes. The "great dumb monsters" of hills frown upon you from the opposite side of the valley—the river flashes along the brown fields; and whilst you are gazing, a fiery courser, harnessed to a cumbrous train of carriages, rushes out of the throat of the rocks, and with mighty galloping, tears the huge length of his burden after him, and vanishes, amongst deep cuttings and overhanging trees, out of your sight. Then you come upon shady nooks and 'tiny glades,' as Tom Miller calls them; and all around you, through the woody openings, the sunlight bursts in gorgeous streams over the blue-bells, and white starry flowers, and golden kingcups. Here is a wild gooseberry bush growing, full of berries—and hark! how the music gushes out of the throat of that startled blackbird. A dog barks in the neighbouring wood, and that double-barrelled fire has carried death to some one or more of Nature's speechless children.

We now come to a break in the wood—the bushes are few and scattered, and upon a green platform, rising over the dell below, which we must presently cross, there are some fine stately trees. On the left hand of the platform, with Clifton village for a back ground, you may perceive a coal-pit with its iron wheels and smoky chimney. There is a ruined water dam in the field, just before you come to the coal-pit, beside which a cow is feeding. At the bottom of the dell runs a small railway, upon which the coal is conveyed from the pit to a wharf by the road side. When the carriages are full, they run down to the wharf by their own weight, and the impetus of descent; they are then drawn back by the engine. See, there are a man and a boy leaning over the rails below, waiting to receive a cargo of coals for their craft, which is • now lying moored in the Calder. After crossing this dell, you still continue your course upon the hill top, making your way through the trees and tangled underwood as well as you can, and seeing at intervals, all the various scenes which present themselves there. At the end of this wood the land in the valleys is getting arable—and yonder is a veritable hay stack, with a heap of lime close by it, and a water cart painted red, flung on its stern sheets, as an old Salt would say, with the shafts turned up, upon which a chain hangs. We will descend the hill here, and leave the wood for the high road, not forgetting to quench our thirst with the water which issues midway down the hill from a rocky cavern.

Now after all this walking and talking we have not advanced above a mile from Brighouse; for looking back we can see the church, houses, factories, and the strong dark hills on the other side of them. We are not far, however, from Kirklees, and still nearer to Clifton, where we will go and dine. The path is flagged all the way to Cooper Bridge, and the scenery upon the road looks as beautiful, I think, as it did awhile ago from the hill top. Look there are three villanous school-boys, who have seated themselves by a stone-heap on the road side (for it is Saturday afternoon), and not knowing what to

do with themselves, are pulling up the grass
and pelting one another.   Now they are cuffing
and tumbling, and laughing as boys can laugh;
and now one has thrown himself all his length
on the green sward, and lies there kicking up
his heels, in an excess of joy and merriment.

We, that is thou, and I, O reader! will turn
up this lane to the left, and go, as I said before,
and dine at the "*Black Horse*" in Clifton.   We
must not forget, however, when we arrive at the
top of the lane, to turn round and survey the
landscape.   It is of no use to tell you what sort
of a landscape it is, for I am tired of these descriptions.   I will only advise you then to go and
see it.   The entrance to Clifton is both wild and
beautiful, especially in the spring, for the gardens
are all blooming then with rich apple blossom,
and through the fine orchard trees we get
glimpses of the valley, lying far below us.   We
pass some huge stone-quarries on the left hand,
and the next turn of the road brings us to the
"Black Horse,"—one of Izaak Walton's "Way-
side Inns," with "lavender in the window, and
twenty ballads stuck about the walls."   And
here I will promise you such good entertainment,
as to use another Waltonism, is fit for none but
"honest men."   So, reader! if thou be a rogue,
do not call at the "*Black Horse.*"

When you leave this good old fashioned Inn,
enquire the way to Kirklees Park.   Directly
you are clear of the village, it rises before you

with its gorgeous trees, stretching far away. Keep the road until you come to a green gate on the left hand side. This is the chief Park Gate, and leads past the Ice-house through a beautiful avenue, up to the Porter's Lodge, and thence to the old hall of Sir George Armitage. At that lodge-door you may knock if you like, and send a messenger from amongst the inmates to ask permission for you to walk along the terrace to Robin Hood's Grave. Then pass boldly down by the lodge side, and take the first turn to the left, which will lead you to the terrace.

And here, all language would fail to convey any idea of the scenery which bursts upon us from the beautiful wooded platform upon which we have entered. Far below us lie the woods of Kirklees, for we are on the very top of the terrace which Nature has formed here, walking amongst lofty trees, whose rich foliage seems to inlay the azure of heaven as we look up at them. On one side of us stands the Hall, with its fine broad park, which is fenced off from the terrace, and in which herds of deer are cropping the rich grass. On the other side lie those interminable mountains, and all the unspeakable glories of the valley. And here we walk along for a good mile, occasionally resting on the rustic seats which are placed so as to command the finest prospects, until at last we come to the noblest seat, inlaid with wood at the back in the shape of diamond pannels, and the noblest prospect of all. It is close to Robin's grave, and is the highest point of that mighty table land.

I will confess to have had the strangest emotions when I first stood over the remains of this old forest hero. With all my Sherwood associations, and such historical, traditional, and ballad recollections as lay within me, I stood there, and had no words, nor can I now find any, to tell what my feelings were, nor my thoughts. Brave-hearted Robin! Thou, at least, hast a fitting resting-place, in this glorious park, amongst these solemn yews, and silent trees. Farewell!

HIS EPITAPH:—

" Here underneath this laist steun
Laz, robert, Earl of Huntingdon.
Ne'er archers wer az hie sa geud
An pipl kauld im robin heud.
Sich outlawz az hi an iz men
Wil England niver si agen.

"Obiit 24 Kal: De Kembris, 1247."

When the "Princess" had done reading this long account of Robin Hood and the old Forest, she dropped the book, and would have fallen asleep, I do believe, from exhaustion and some thing else, if the good Rector had not presented her with a glass of foaming Champagne. Our friend the sculptor, who is a man of ponderous dimensions, and seems to have been fashioned after the model of the " *Major Oak*,"—which, as already stated, is ninety feet in circumference, at six inches from the ground—was quite angry at the infliction she had undergone, and proposed that she should eat a " continent of beef," and drink a " Mediterranean sea of brewis," to restore her. He, however, was thinking of the repairs which his own ample corporation would have required in a like case, and forgot that the wing of a lark is enough for a fair lady.

John Trueman—who is a little man, about five feet five inches in stature, with a broad and lofty forehead, over which his black hair stands erect, and a pair of large dark eyes in his head, which are at once merry and thoughtful— laughed heartily, at the Sculptor's conceit, and kept the whole party in a roar for some time, with his quaint remarks upon it.

It is worth anything to hear John laugh. I have heard many good laughers, and once saw Thomas Carlyle take hold of a gate-post, in the pastures near Rawden, and shake it like a reed, in a real horse-fit of laughter, over a tale I was telling him about old John, the Sherwood Theologian, who loved the wars of the " bloody Jews," a good deal better than the " dry stuff" contained in the new Testament; and who, on being asked by the clergyman whether he " believed," answered, " O to be sure I do, sir ! to be sure I do. I believe in the Father, Son, and Holy Ghost, and all the whole kit on 'um, sir ;" and who further replied, when the parson told him he was sorry to find him so dark, and benighted in spiritual matters, "Dark, sir! dark, sir! dark be d—d, sir! I can see as well as you can!"—I say I have heard Carlyle laugh, but Trueman outlaughs him, and all other men I have yet met with. Not only the muscles of his face—but his eyes, arms, legs, right away down to the great toes, shake and quiver, as if in mortal throes, and his hair shoots out electric streams, making it dangerous for nervous people to approach him at such times.

As soon as order was restored, I called upon John to give us a short history of the entymology of the Forest, which he did in a very interesting manner, and told us the haunts, nature, habits, and metamorphosis, of the various insects and butterflies, which peopled the invisible worlds around us—that is to say, the dark holes in the trees, the moss, grass, ferns, and foliage. For John knows every insect that flies, and can tell you their whole genealogy, and what will become of some of them when they die; which is more than he can tell of himself, or me.

On dark nights he goes into the Forest with a a pot of rum and honey which he smears over the bark of the trees, to lure the insects he wishes to take. After waiting some time, he pulls a dark lanthern from his pocket, and throws the light full upon the tree, where he beholds his victims enjoying their death-supper,

with no small satisfaction. He then quietly
brushes them into a tin box, which he carries
with him for that purpose, and kills them with
spirits of camphor. In this and other ways
—he has got together one of the rarest
cabinets in the kingdom. So he told us, as we
sat under the branches of the " Major Oak"—
and as it was his turn to call upon some one to
add to the afternoon's entertainment, he desired
our friend the Sculptor, to sing Spencer Hall's
song, beginning, " O ! the fern-clad hills of
Sherwood," the music to which he, the said
Sculptor, had composed. After a good deal of
grunting—and complaints of hoarseness—he
pitched his pipes somewhere about as low as
double Z., and sang the following song :—

" O ! the fern-clad hills of Sherwood,
  How beautiful are they ;
When morning hangs on dappled wing
  Calling the dews away !
I love to bound along their tops,
  When breezes mild, though free,
Play o'er the bloomy fields below,
  And bear their sweets to me!

" O ! the woody plains of Sherwood,
  Outspreading far and wide,
Where peeps the low, pretenceless cot,
  The palace towers in pride :
How glorious 'tis to wander there
  When the mid-day lark upsprings,
A tiny speck in the boundless sky,
  That with its music rings !

"O! the deep, lone dells of Sherwood,
  So quiet and sublime,
Where with the wood bird's mellow voice
  Is heard the streamlet's chime :
How sweet the winding paths to thread
  When twilight's tender hour
Subdues and melts the musing heart
  Yet gives the spirit power !

" Dear native scenes of Sherwood—all !
  Hill, woodland, plain, and dell,
I view ye with a lover's eye,
  A lover's heart as well !
For from my boyhood's joyous hours
  Hath it been mine to roam
Amongst you far away, yet still
  Feel everywhere at home !"

The ladies were delighted with this song, and
the good Mater said "it was just like Spencer
Hall."

"Ah !" answered the Rector, "if the old
fellow were only with us to-day, our happiness
would be complete."

"Never mind, dear Pater," said Miss M.,
"for so long as his friends love him, he can
never be absent from them."

"True," rejoined the Princess, "love is the
only thing which makes me feel sure of the
immortality of the soul."

Upon which I saw the Quaker turn suddenly,
and look the beautiful speaker in the face, as if
she had uttered his deepest conviction. He said
nothing, however, but drew his little daughter
close up to his heart ; and I knew that he was
deeply moved, for he had suffered great bereave-

ments, and his love for the dead was eternal.——
No one else, however, noticed my friend's emotion; and as the wine went merrily round, Christopher Thompson was asked to describe some
"pleasant spots, and retired nooks," in Sherwood,
before we broke up our party for a ramble
through the Forest.

"Well," said Christopher, "you have heard
Birkland and Bilhaugh described in the paper
read by Her Royal Highness, the 'Princess.'
The Forest itself is now about seven or eight
miles in length, and varying from two to three
miles in breadth, scattered over with patriarchal oaks, whose peers are not to be found in
any other part of our island. Many of the trees
have, at this late day, acquired local names—
either from their peculiarity of form, or from
their association with good men. Here are
a few of them:——The Parliament Oak, the
Major Oak, the Millhouse Oak, the Green Dale
Oak, the Duke's Walking-stick, &c."

BUDBY FOREST.

"In the north-eastern corner of Birkland,"
continued Christopher, "lies that wild moorland
tract called Budby Forest, as wild as the ardent
lover of unpruned nature can desire, barring the
formal hunting-drives that occasionally intersect
it. This part of the Forest is clear of the oaks,
and other large timber trees, that adorn old Bilhaugh; but it is studded over with broad, low-

crowned hawthorns, that, in the latter May
time, or early June, are powdered over with
white clustering blossoms, which flood the wilderness with aroma; spreading over miles in length,
lovely as a blushing maiden on her bridal, and
present a picture rarely to be found. They are picturesque in all seasons, spangling the green-sward
with their tender shadows in the sunny Summer-
time; splendid when Autumn throws around
them her gorgeous season-tints, transformed
by her golden touch into every conceivable hue,
from rusty green to pure vermillion; and when
the storms of Winter have begun their denuding
sport, these hawthorns present a charming contrast, with their dark-brown stems and twigs,
all festooned with druidical wreaths of deep-
green, shining mistletoe, spotted with white
viscid berries. The Forest is variegated with
countless undying-green gorse shrubs, which
in the Spring-time and Autumn, are all golden
with papillonaceous blossoms; an ocean of
beauty, whose golden billows heave to the
nectar-bearing breezes, as far as the eye can
reach. Here the linnets, winchats, blackbirds,
and silver-piped thrushes, are singing gladsome
strains before morning unbars the gates of light,
and their music is continued as grey twilight
spreads the soft couch of even; not a sound,
save of Nature's choristers, breaks the repose
of this ' wilderness of sweets.' Occasionally a
flock of black-faced forest sheep may be seen

tracking their way, nibbling the gorse as they go along—and sometimes the old shepherd, mounted on his grey, shaggy donkey, or leading him by the bridle, goes plodding after them.—On the eastern border of the Forest, you approach the pleasant village of Budby, by a turnpike road which leads from Ollerton to Worksop. A castle crowns the hill-top, and looks over the village, which lies at its feet.—War, however, forms no part of the castle's business; the four circular towers which decorate the angles do not fear any disruption of their cement from the roar of brass or iron 'bull-dogs,' in their embrasures, nor their parapets from a flank of bowmen, unless perchance some 'keeper' should here marshal himself, to throw a shaft at the sleek, antlered deer, which are browsing on the hill-side: nor is the flag-staff in fear of a long shot, whilst signalling the approach of an enemy; sufficient for him if he flaunts his crimson on such rare occurrences as a royal progress, or the still more rare one of a royal visit to Sherwood. This castle is indeed one of peace, dispelling fear by its picturesque beauty—

———' hath a pleasant seat; the air
Humbly and sweetly recommends itself
Unto our gentle senses!'

" This village usually wins the approbation of

G

the traveller from its quiet and neat appearance;
several of the cottages are really picturesque, in
the Elizabethian style, rose-clustered and surrounded with comfortable garden-plots.   The
river Meden adds his charms · as he babbles
through this village, now leaping and foaming
over the twisted root of an old willow, now
shouting as he bounds around the turn of a
sedgy bank, then stealing away so softly,—a
broad expanse of silver gliding toward the fine
lake of Thorsby.   This sweet forest stream
abounds with wild-fowl, which here enjoy the
peaceful silence of the place, broken only by
song-birds, or the majestic voyaging of the
graceful swan.   The village is the property of
Earl Manvers, and you may journey very far
ere you find one where the cottagers enjoy more
of domestic quiet and rural beauty, than may be
found in the cottage-homes of Budby."

"Ah!" cried the ladies, "let us go and visit
Budby Forest.   This is the pleasant month of
June, and the white thorns must now be in full
blossom."

"Do not be in a hurry," quoth the Rector;
"perhaps our friend Thompson can introduce
us to one or two more of his pleasant nooks."

"With all my heart," said Christopher.
"Here is a visit to 'Clipstone Castle' and 'St.
Edwin's Chapel,' which I wrote a long while
ago, for a little periodical formerly published at
Edwinstowe, called the '*Sherwood Gatherer.*'

CLIPSTONE CASTLE AND ST. EDWIN'S CHAPEL.

"A sunny morning last month lured me into the fields, and I strolled along the banks of the chittering river Maun, communing with the ferns, making posy-pictures of the ladysmocks, golden-cupped ranunculuses, pearl-eyed daisies, and the endless beautiful flowers that spangled its green border. I was soon reminded by a white-barred gate, which for a moment forced me to leave my floral grouping, that I must become common-place for awhile; being within ken of the ancient dames that in yonder porched and benched cottages of Clipstone, were exchanging a morning's village gossip. —Bang!—The clap of that gate is mimic thunder in this peaceful spot. All again is silent—still as the world's first morning—not a sound save the soft plaint of the winds—the whimpering of the stream, and the music of the warblers who from every bough and grassy mead are trilling songs of cheerfulness to the God of all goodness. Hark, that loud halloo!—'tis the laugh of happy children that are rolling over each other, 'a merry heap,' on yon mossy bank—down they go, over and over, now up again—the newly-breeched urchin fain would climb the guide-post, but he has 'too much pudding' in his corduroys—ha! laugh again! How they rollick upon the mossy carpet—hark ye! echo shouts, laugh again! Happy souls! may your riper years be as full of comfort, as your sunny hours of childhood.

"Yon crumbling mass of ruins that crowns the hill, is the remains of Clipstone Palace, once the favourite abode of royalty. The Norman Conqueror claimed Clipstone Park, amongst the many others, in his whole-sale confiscation of English Parks. In Clipstone Castle the lion-hearted Crusader, the first Richard, enter-tained the King of Scots in 1194. John frequently re-sided and held courts here. In this bowery nook of 'merrie Shirewood,' the fickle king felt himself secure. To this day the village tradition assigns this castle to that pale-heart, and speaks of it as King John's Palace. Here, with bowmen, retainers, and the usual train of lip-serving courtiers, he could smother conscience for the moment, and chase the bounding deer, in Birkland's glades: no stern-hearted barons to perplex him —no vision of the Charter of English Rights, no daydream of Runnymede, to mar his pleasure,—here he was 'every inch a king.' He cared not for excommunicating Popes, or wily Pandolphs.

"The first Edward occasionally visited at this Castle; and the second Edward, according to the Chronicles, held his Christmas there in 1315, and 1316, not only for the pleasure of the chase, but, if possible, to catch

> "' Him—that prince of archers—Robin Hood—
> And his brave knot of gallant Sherwood-men,
> Whose peers those glades shall never greet again.'

"Edward III. made Clipstone Castle an occasional residence; Henry VI., on the 20th of March, 1422, granted a charter to Nottingham and Clipstone Palace. In 1514, the royal bigamist Henry VIII., granted Clipstone Park to his Lord Treasurer, Thomas, Earl of Surrey, when he made him Duke of Norfolk. The property once more reverted to the crown, and in James the First's time, it was granted to Gilbert, Earl of Shrewsbury. This ancient domain, supposed to be the oldest in England, is now the property of the Duke of Portland, who preserves, with laudable pride, the remains of the ancient pile to whisper its stories of the olden time to all visitors. The once-vaulted walls now present a mass of crumbling rubble; and scarcely a trace of architecture remains. Only three faced stones are left, which appear to have formed a part of a stone staircase. A corbel stone, on which is carved a bluff-cheeked image with a crown on its head, grins upon the angle of a one-storied cottage close by, as if in mockery of the royal ruins before it. Traces of the moat are still visible, and village crones talk of long subterranean passages, and the dire sounds that have issued thence, like to the moan of captive knights and the shriek of pining ladies; whilst strange sights they say of spectre figures, make the 'night hideous.'

"The last man who held the title of King's Huntsman for the hays of Birkland and Bilhaugh, was, a generation ago, laid in a green grave in the churchyard of Edwinstewe; the dog-kennels are changed into cottages, and the imagination fills up the void with dim visions of a dim age. Neat, trelliced, rose-entwined, and comfort-breathing cottages, are picturesquely dotted around the castle, and reflected in the clear and limpid stream that steals through the pleasant village of Clipstone.

"Near to the Palace of Clipstone stood the Chapel of St. Edwine. A few moss-grown stones are all that mark the spot where the holy father, from the palace, was wont to offer up the mass for the kingly train who there held court. The plough has upturned the site—the mighty oaks, that spread their sturdy arms over the sacred retreat, have long ago yielded to the woodman's axe; the shrine, with its emblems of devotion, is mouldering in the dust, and wild flowers bloom upon the spot where the penitent knelt to tell his beads.

> " ' But as the dewy wind blows sweetly by,
> Upon the thoughtful listener's joyful ear
> Doth come a sweet and holy symphony—
> And Nature's choristers are chaunting masses high,' "

We all thanked Christopher for his wee bits of history, and the Rector, picking up one of the little volumes, which lay upon the grass be-

G 3

side him, called "*The Foresters' Offering*," by Spencer T. Hall, volunteered to read a page or two from that delightful book.

Perhaps the reader may require to be told who Spencer Hall is; and I will tell him.—He is a man belonging to the same class of poets at the head of which stands Clare and Bloomfield. He was born at Brookside Cottage, in Sutton-in-Ashfield, of poor, but respectable parents, who are members of the Society of Friends. At an early age he ran away from his home, to York, I believe, and through the influence of some friend, was bound apprentice to a printer in that city. His education had been much neglected during his youth, and he now resolved to spend all his leisure time in self-instruction. Before his indentures were out, he had acquired a respectable education; and made himself acquainted, to some extent, with the literature of his country. He soon after begun to write himself, and the result of his early efforts is contained in "*The Forester's Offering.*" This book is remarkable because he printed it himself, and composed the pieces in it without committing them to paper. He soon after published another volume, called "*Rambles in the Country,*" which attracted some notice amongst the lovers of country scenery. We next find him in business for himself, as a Bookseller and Printer, in Sutton-in-Ashfield; and some years later he was appointed Governor of

Hollis Hospital, in Sheffield.   About this time his attention was directed to Mesmerism, and Phrenology; and finding that he had great mesmeric power, and that in the course of his experiments, he educed some very remarkable psychological manifestations, he resolved to devote himself entirely to these subjects—and began his career as a public lecturer upon them.   He subsequently resigned his situation at Hollis Hospital, and became the most noted man of his time, in the department he had chosen.

The poor Quaker boy was now a visitor at the houses of the nobility, and while he was at Pall Mall, in London, the highest personages in the kingdom were sometimes kept waiting in his anti-chamber, before they could be admitted into his august presence.   His next essay in literature was the publication of a little periodical called " The Phreno-Magnet," and shortly afterwards appeared his " Mesmeric Experiences."   The most remarkable circumstance in Hall's mesmeric history, was his cure of Harriet Martineau, the celebrated writer of political novels and travels, of a disease of long standing, which had confined her for years to her sitting-room, and compelled her to the use of opium and other powerful stimulants.   The cure was so successful that Miss M. publicly acknowleged it ; and confessed that she was able, after being but a short time under Hall's treatment, to walk a distance of four or five miles without weariness.   Our friend Spencer, feeling that his mesmeric mission is completed, has now taken up his residence in South Shields.   He has lately published a little volume of poems, and a book upon Ireland, recording therein his own experience of the people and country during a recent visit which he made to the sister island.   In personal appearance he is rather prepossessing; and his manners are polished and unassuming. No one, however, can have any idea of the man, by seeing him upon the platform, or in public company.   It is only in the retirement of private life, that his virtues and talents are set off to advantage.   Beyond the restraint of the fashionable drawing-room he is a warm and gentle companion; full of fun and good nature; loves a hearty laugh; and occasionally an uproarious hurrah; quotes poetry, and perpetrates puns in the same breath; and can leave a serious conversation upon Swedenborg and the immortality of the soul, to play *barber*-ous tricks upon his best friends.   He is a firm believer in the supernatural; and can reconcile ghosts with his philosophy of life and death.   He has a strange revelation yet to make of his mesmeric experiences; and perhaps, when the world is wiser, he will publish them.

And now, good Rector, fill your glass, and let us drink to Hall's health; for although he is a teetotaller (Christopher says, it almost chokes him to get the word out!) he would not refuse to be pledged by so good a company. There, now then begin.   Whereupon the Rector reads aloud a passage describing

THE FOREST IN THE OLDEN TIMES.

" WHAT a magnificent forest must this have been in its primeval wildness and luxuriance !   Comprising nearly all of Nottinghamshire, north of the Trent, besides several considerable outstretchings into the neighbouring county of Derby, it could have contained little less originally than one hundred thousand acres of the most harmoniously diversified scenery in England. Even in this late day, it would be difficult to point out in England a similar space, where undulating downs, dusky groves, and strips of fresh green meadow—with here and there some heaven-hued gleam of lake or stream among,—are more beautifully blended in one vast scene, than may be viewed from several eminences on our western and northern borders.   And these again are diversified by numerous intersertions of the 'stately tower or palace fair,' the clustering hamlet, or lonely farm, and all hemmed in by circle beyond circle of dim and distant wolds :—whilst in the more central parts, groups of hoary oaks are the only relief to the eye, on the surface of heaths, whose limits are the blue haze of the horizon.

" There is also a striking uniquity of character in the country running along the south-western boundary, with which I have known even continental tourists peculiarly charmed.   You have probably never heard of the Groves of Kirkby; but it is a spot not less beautiful because it happens to be obscure.   This little remnant of faery-land, you might pass at one hundred yards distance, and see or know nothing of it, unless your attention chanced to be directed to it by some one familiar with the neighbourhood.

"Descending from the rural spire-crowned village of Kirkby by a steep foot-path, and crossing the infant river Erewash, which there winds along with a dove-like murmur, you come to the Mansfield and Pinxton Railway—an unpoetical object truly; but the streams and fields around were never less fresh or green to me for its existence; on the contrary, the sweet contrast of the solitude into which we are about to plunge is agreeably heightened by the sudden transition. Occasionally glancing back at the fine view down Erewash Dale, so beautifully enriched by the woodlands of Langton and Brookhill, you must now climb a steep bank, which, I am sorry to say, has been shorn lately of a most exuberant covering of nut-bushes. Having reached the top of this bank, and proceeded a few yards onwards, in nearly a straight line, veer a little to the right till you come to a row of bushes, and then take care of yourself; otherwise you fall into a wild, woody, and streamy hollow, with precipitous sides, overrun with ivy, woodbine, and various other luxuriant climbers, and sending up—if in Spring-time—the warblings of the brooklets, the whispering of the breeze among its foliage, and the voices of a hundred happy birds, in one loud, thrilling, harmonious hymn, from the midst of its cool and shady depths. As you seek a less abrupt descent into the heart of this fairy dell, you will, perhaps, be startled, whilst indulging in a feeling of absolute loneliness, and remoteness from all human habitations, by the crowing of a cock, or the voice of some other domestic animal, in your immediate vicinity; and, on searching for its whereabouts, you will be surprised to find yourself almost close to a house, and a fine old cluster of farm-buildings, with all the usual concomitances of a prosperous English agricultural establishment.

"After luxuriating on the charms of this beautiful, quiet scene, to your own satisfaction, you may next climb the opposing acclivity, whence your eye will dilate on one of the loveliest landscapes which the mind can imagine. So sensible was some great man in former times of the advantages of this noble position, that he commenced building a mansion in the field where I now suppose you to be standing, which Tradition (who is a favourite old friend of mine) says was on a scale not less magnificent, or extensive, than that of Belvoir Castle—an assertion well confirmed by the lines of its foundations, still traceable. The only vestige of this splendid abortion, however, now perceptible above ground, is the grey and solitary remnant of a very thick wall, near the middle of the field, which as near as I can remember was, when I last measured it, about twenty yards in length, and three in height. On this extraordinary subject history is very brief. The only allusion to it in Thoroton is as follows, without any date being given :—

" ' Sir Charles Cavendish began to build a great house in this lordship (Kirkby), on a hill, by the forest-side, near Annesley Woodhouse, where, being assaulted by Sir John Stanhope and his man, as he was viewing the work, he resolved to leave off his building, because some blood had been spilt in the quarrel, which was then very hot between these two families.'

" Leaving this melancholy monument of feudal animosity by the farm-house I have mentioned, you come, in a walk of about half a mile, to the ridge of those wild, grey, ferny uplands—Robin Hood's Hills—over which, most probably, Washington Irving has already taken you, in his delightful reminiscences of Newstead Abbey. You have rested on the top—you have gazed again and again on the countless hamlets, halls, cottages, and spires, which stud the beautiful, far-stretching, western landscape, to where it closes with the sky, up amid the Peaks of Derbyshire ; and you have recognised the old farm-house at Grives, sending its long, long wreath of blue smoke, gracefully upcurling in the still, pure sunshine below you. But now, having lingered long and lovingly, and rested sufficiently, you approach an old gate on the opposite side of the road,

and the first object that now catches your sight is a
bold, dark, yet distant plantation of pines, directly
fronting you; in it you perhaps descry the dim form
of some half-revealed tower, or turret, and so are induced to scan it more minutely; but as your eye
gradually returns, and you quietly gather in the inter-
mediate scenery, you are astonished to find yourself
gazing into a wild, extensive, amphitheatrical valley,
utterly different in every feature from all you have been
contemplating before,—so adorned with venerable
grandeur, so filled with ancient gloom; and a strange,
solemn thrill runs through your frame, whilst you
whisper to your own heart, that this is the valley of
Byron's Newstead."

"There," said the Rector," as he stopped
suddenly, and looked round him to see if his
audience was weary, "that is what I call a nice
piece of descriptive scenery. And if you are
not tired, I will read one more extract, and
then make way for any one else who may be
disposed to entertain you."

I besought the good Rector to drink a glass of
Burgundy, thinking that his throat must be dry,
after so much reading; and we all assured him,
we should like to hear the passage he proposed
to read.

"Well then," said he, pushing the bottle
under my nose, as he drained his glass, "we
have heard the south-western border of Sherwood described, and we will now go to the

SOUTH-EASTERN BORDER OF THE FOREST.

"What rich combinations of rural scenery, too,

along the south-eastern border, from Nottingham down-wards ! There the silvery Trent uncoils itself in the centre of a vast pastoral plain, and speeds along now with a graceful curve—now with a majestic sweep ; where in some places the woods run down to its very margin, and almost dip their foreheads in its flood ; and in others, stretch serenely, yet solemnly, away up the gentle slopes to the landscape's verge, whilst occasion-ally some fair rocket-like spire, as at Gedling, rises into the clear, blue heavens from their umbrageous bosoms ! And then, as we quit the neighbourhood of the river, what unexpected and enchanting acquaintance we find ourselves cultivating with Nature, and in her wild soli-tudes at Lambley Dumbles, so pleasantly and graphi-cally described by Thomas Miller, in his 'Royston Gower ;' and still further on, in the neighbourhood of Rainworth Waters, Oxton Grange, and Grave's Lane ! —scenes which always fill me with the same rich, deep feelings, as those inspired by reading the solitary and sublime wanderings of Derwent Conway ! And yet, continuing in the same direction, towards the quiet little clerical town of Southwell, with its noble old cathedral gleaming over the verdant champaign, what a noble succession of beauties gladden the eye and the heart, as we loiter on where the chrystal Grete makes cool, tinkling music, as if it trotted along on silver feet, in the quivering shade of its sunlit border-trees. But it is down in the far

NORTH-EASTERN DISTRICTS

that man has made the least havoc with the rights of Nature. There it is that we read the genesis of her glorious book, not as altered or translated by art, but in the bold, original, and sublime characters of her own revealing ! There, where the waters of the Rainworth, the Man, the Menden, the Poulter, the Wollen, and

H

other forest streams, flow towards each other through the glades, as to some grand convocation of the River-god, blending their voices with the solemn hymns of the woods on their way—there, where the palace of our ancient kings, at Clipstone, is crumbling in its last decay, and near where that of a still earlier line of monarchs vanished, ages before—where the venerable abbies of Rufford and Welbeck, centuries ago, shuffled off their original character, and became transformed into seats of most aristocratical luxury and magnificence—and in the immediate neighbourhood too, of Thoresby and Clumber—gorgeous modern palaces— (especially the latter) outrivaling all our conceptions of Italian profusion and taste—there, amongst all these impressive tokens of unceasing change, stand, in their primitive grandeur and glory, the hills and woods which Nature reared in the Forest as a home for the out-lawed patriot, Robin Hood, before she herself elected him king over the whole of this wide and wonderful sylvan domain."

And here the Rector closed the book, when the fair Mater asked, how far Thoresby and Clumber were from the Major Oak.

"Thoresby," said Christopher, "which is the seat of Earl Manners, and is surrounded by noble parks, full of deer, with a wide lake close to it, is about five miles off; and Clumber, the seat of the Duke of Newcastle, is about eight. Both lie within the Forest; and so does Welbeck-Hall, about six miles off, the seat of the Duke of Portland. We foresters," he continued, "call these districts the 'Dukeries,' although we like Nature's coronets better than theirs, a good deal."

"And Rufford Abbey?" enquired the Mater, "Where is that?"

"Three miles off, perhaps," answered Christopher," on the other side of Edwinstowe. By the way, there is a little bit in the '*Forester's Offering*,' about Rufford, which, if you will permit me, I will read to you."

"Certainly" said we, "read on."

"It is very short," said Christopher, "and runs thus."

"But what a charming day we have been enjoying at Rufford Abbey! Don't you remember it all—and the little incident by the road too? There was the old woman in a man's coat, and a slouched bonnet, with a bundle of sticks on her head, a great rotten hedge stake in her hand, and a short black pipe stuck between her teeth. And then the dark-eyed young gipsey, who wanted to tell our fortunes, in that green lane, by the old wood-side, near to where we sat and read the Woodman's Tale! to say nothing of the chubby urchin who, —being hired to frighten birds away, had left a field of ripe wheat, at the mercy of half a dozen flocks of hungry sparrows,—had laid his dinner-wallet, and clapper down on the road side, and was enjoying himself with a sly game at pitch-and-hustle, with an itinerant little sweep, and a truant school-boy; while the sweep's half famished terrier was as slily regaling herself with a clandestine rummage among the contents of the wallet! You remember all these things, as we saw them before we entered that magnificent avenue of beeches—those living colonades which so gracefully supported lofty arches of rich foliage under the cloudless blue! And you can never forget what we afterwards saw about the Abbey itself:—The numerous artizans in the court, all plying their skill for the improvement of that immense and irregular fabric; the development of appropriate *character* in the kitchen, where cooks and scullions were busy; and among whom the athletic keeper, Brock, marched in such fine old English style, with a landing net over his shoulder, charged with as prime a pike as ever an ancient Abbot of Rufford fasted upon in Lent; a rare group for Landseer!—the vast cellars, into which long streaks of light were sent, through old monastic gratings, upon huge barrels of from fifty to five hundred and fifty gallons each, amongst which ranged a man with a can and glass. and such a rosy face, as betokened nothing discreditable to the cheer he dealt out; the capacious Gothic servant's hall, with its wide, old-fashioned hearth, upon which we looked, and almost felt the comfort and gleesomeness of a long Christmas-night in such a place;—the long-drawn gallery, with half-closed shutters, where hung the dim pictures of an age as dim;—the vast 'brick-hall,' with its massy oaken organ-gallery, and carved oaken skreen; and the look-out thence, through quaint, ancient windows, upon ancient, and mystic trees;—the look and the talk of *comfort* in the housekeeper's room; and the personification of comfort and good management, in the housekeeper herself; the affecting melancholy smile of poor, gentle, Jenny C——e, who bore a striking resemblance to the reason-reft Maria of Sterne, as she led her faithful little dog about the house, with an evident consciousness that toleration and kindness, were no strangers there;—and finally, the frank hospitality of the steward's room.   You remember all this, and confessed with me, as we came away along the border of the beautiful lake, which stretches out from before the Abbey into the woods, that each scene we had beheld, was like a stanza of some rare and complete descriptive poem of the olden time, which it was delightful to read, and impossible to forget."

" Bravo Spencer!" said the Rector, when

Christopher had done reading, "We must go and see that abbey to-morrow, and as many of the other notorieties of Sherwood as we can, beside. But I am afraid the ladies must be tired with sitting so long, and propose that we take a turn up the Forest glades."

To this we all agreed; and the servants were requested to prepare a cup of tea for us by the time we returned. Now I like tea—not weak tea, however, which always makes me think of the "Edinburgh Review's" criticism upon James Montgomery's poems, wherein the poet is set down as a " young man much addicted to weak tea and female society;" and for this reason, especially when ladies are present, I prefer a strong decoction of the delicious herb. And after all that I have said in favour of Burgundy, I would rather be deprived of this and every other wine, than relinquish my cup of tea. For you must know, that notwithstanding appearances are against me in this book, I am not a toper, but, for the most part, a cold-water drinker, and in my tea drinking propensities, almost an old woman of eighty! I like the exhilarating influence which a cup of rich congou spreads over the nervous system. A rough, wiry flavour, that sticks to the palate like old Port, is my delight. Leigh Hunt is for a choicer drink, and recommends the following mixture, viz.—a quarter of a pound of Souchong, two ounces of gunpowder, or young hyson, and an ounce of orange pekoe. I have tried it, and think it "choicely good," but green tea is too exciting for my nerves; and hence I avoid it. Two hours after tea, are the most delightful time of the day to me; and are always spent in my study. I have a habit of carrying off my last cup, and sipping it there alone; much to the annoyance of my wife, who sometimes finds half her tea-service, (the accumulation of several days' delinquencies) buried amongst piles of books and papers; and I assure you she very rarely forgets, on such occasions, to scold me for persisting in this inveterate habit.

Well, I remained behind a moment to admonish the servants not to drown us with water instead of tea, and whilst the Foresters (Christopher, Trueman, and Widdison) went to look for firewood—promising to follow directly, I ran after our friends. Coming up to Miss M. and her governess, I found they were examining some beautiful mosses which they had gathered by the way.

"Ah!" I said, "you have soon discovered some of the hidden treasures of the Forest; and I congratulate you upon your microscopic eyes and fine taste. There are I know not how many varieties of moss in this old realm; and the ferns grow more gracefully, and arrive at a fuller maturity here than anywhere else."

"I should much like to preserve a few specimens," said Miss M—, "in remembrance of this charming visit ; and, perhaps, you will help us to gather them."

"With all my heart," said I. "Just come with me over this dingle, and, I will shew you the most curious, if not the most beautiful, specimen of moss, in the Forest."

"With that we wandered up to our knees (for ladies have *knees* in England, although the leg does not extend higher than the *ankle* in America; and an American lady would never forgive you, if you ventured to hint of a more extensive latitude in that direction) I say we wandered knee-deep in heather and ferns, over a little dingle hard by, until we came to the stumps of several oak trees, which had been felled by the woodman.

"Now stoop down, young ladies," I said, "and behold what a cluster of singular mosses is here."

They did so; and their fairy fingers were soon busily engaged in plucking the stems from their roots.—Let me explain what kind of mosses they are. I forget—indeed never heard the botanical name for them—but the Foresters call them the "sealing-wax mosses." They do not grow anywhere but upon the stumps of trees, and consist of little flat stems, about an inch long, of a grey colour, having their tops covered with a red pigment, like a drop of sealing-wax ; hence their name.

The ladies gathered a quantity of this pretty

moss; and as we were leaving the dell, a nightingale burst out in such rich, melodious strains, that we stayed to listen, being both surprised and delighted at so sudden and unexpected a pleasure.

When we came up with our friends, we found the Foresters had joined them; and in the glade leading down to the open common before the village, we saw a troop of young men and women, dressed in their holiday attire, coming to meet us.

"Ho! ho!" said Christopher and Widdison, in the same breath, "here come our lads and lasses, with their music-books and instruments, to give us a concert in the Forest, I suppose."

"Capital!" cried the Quaker; and everybody was pleased at this mark of honour and attention—this earnest desire to make us happy, and the day memorable.

We stopped till they came up; and having exchanged a hearty welcome, Christopher requested them to await our return at the Major Oak. We then wandered through Bilhaugh, that "ruined Palmyra of the forest," as Pemberton calls it, with its mighty and desolate oaks, already described in the paper read by the "Princess." We afterwards returned up the great Riding, which divides Bilhaugh from Birkland; and our friends, who had not seen the Forest before, were much struck by the contrast presented between the oaks and birches.—

The ladies were in raptures at the sight of so many beautiful, silvery-armed creatures, with their long "musical tresses," as the Quaker called them; and they understood, moreover, what he meant by this expression; for the wind murmured through them, with a sound like the voices of the waves on the sea-shore.

When we returned to the Major Oak, we found a goodly company already assembled round the large wood fire, and the kettle boiling in good earnest. The pretty governess and the quiet Mater dispensed the bounties of the tea; whilst we all sat around them in a circle, under the gigantic branches of the friendly tree. And, reader, in order to bear in mind what sort of a tree this is, be good enough, if you have forgotten the fact, to turn to the record of its dimensions. And now, you village musicians, let us have some music over our tea! Sing us Spencer Hall's song of the "Sheep-Shearers;" and do you, John Trueman, join in the praises of your good old father, who, if he were here, would sing and rejoice as heartily as any of us.

SONG.

"The oaks of the Forest
  Their green locks renew—
The busks of the valley
  Their blossomy hue;
The ' sheep all in clusters'
  Are gathering near,
And with gladness we welcome
  The shearing-time here!

H 3

"But when it is over,
    And round our free board
The villagers gather
    Their mirth to unhoard,
Say, who like poor TRUEMAN
    The glee shall prolong,
With ' The Sheep all in Clusters,'
    His favourite song ?

"O ! the leaves of the Forest,
    Though soon they will dim,
And the bloom of the valley
    Be sleeping like him;
Like him, in new glory,
    Again they'll awake ;
While ' The Sheep all in Clusters'
    We sing for his sake."

We were all very well pleased with this song, especially the Foresters, who joined heart and soul in the chorus; for old Trueman was as great a favourite in the village of Edwinstowe, as his son John now is. At the request of the Governess, a song by J. S. was next sung, called the

HUNTING SONG.

" Hark ! the bugle-horn is sounding
    O'er the upland hills away—
Thro' the mist the deer are bounding ;
    Ho ! the scent lies well to-day,
        Slip the dogs ! away ! away !
        Ho ! the scent lies well to-day.

" Mount and follow, huntsman, after ;
    One is turning from the herd.

Forward ride with merry laughter ;
Lagging horses must be spurred.
    Wind the horn ! away ! away !
    Ho ! the scent lies well to day,

" Over brake, and bog, and heather,
Thro' the golden gorse and corn,
We dash onward, thro' all weather,
To the music of the horn.
    Tantive ho ! away ! away !
    The scent, my boys, lies well to-day.

" Hark ! the hounds give tongue so cheerly;
They are on the old deer's track.
See ! the sun shines on him clearly ;
There he goes, with tawny back !
    Tantive, heigho ! tantivy, away !
    The scent, my boys, lies well to-day.

" Now the horn hath ceased its winding—
They have lost the trail, I fear :
Try back ! 'twill be easy finding ;
Try the dell and moorland near.
    Steady ! we shall soon away,
    For the scent lies well to-day.

" There he starts !   Ho ! noble fellow !
From the dell he bounds along;
Mark his haunch, and horns so yellow—
He is fleet as well as strong.
    Sound the horn ! away ! away !
    For the scent lies well to-day.

" Up the hills he hies to cover :
Forward, dogs ! ye ho ! ye ho !
Sweet the scent of hay and clover,
From the pastures, as we go.
    Sound the horn ! away ! away !
    We shall kill a stag to-day.

" Ah ! he winds ! and downward falling,
    Eyes the fierce dogs howling on.
Hark ! the huntsman's loudly calling,
    ' In at death !' the chace is done.
        Sound the horn, and then away,
        For we have killed a stag to-day."

When tea was over, and the musicians were weary of playing and singing, our friend the Quaker, called upon his little daughter to recite a passage from a poem by "one January Searle," he said, called " *The Gala ;*" which she did with very good effect.   Here is the passage ; and the scene described is Kirklees Park, where Robin Hood was buried.   You will get a glimpse here of the old nunnery, from the lodge chamber of which Robin shot his last arrow.

———————————————"Oft had I heard
In Sherwood Forest, by the cottage hearths
Of Edwinstowe, on many a winter night,
Traditions of his death and burial.
And all the scenes which Robin loved so well,
From Cresswell's savage crags, where Wollen rolls,
And Budby's heath, and Birkland's faery realm
Of silver birches, to the ruined oaks
Of Bilhaugh lone and desolate, I know,
And standing there, beside his mouldering bones,
The dews of Sherwood I that morn had brushed
From the dark ling, scarce dry upon my feet ;
I seemed to bring the forest to his manes
With all its wailing memories and trees.

    " Who now will come with me and pay once more
Sad homage at the brave old hero's grave ?
I know the spot which yonder pinetrees hide
Under their sunless gloom ; and we will go
Down to the Porter's Lodge, and mount the heights

Of the Great Terrace, past the seven beech trees,
Where all the vale of Calder lies below,
Soft dreaming with the river in its arms,
Under the shadows of the mighty hills.
No fitter path could lead to such a tomb.
Thick as a forest grow the towering trees,
Thro' which the landscape, in its finest sweeps,
Bursts like the vision of a sudden world.
We tread o'er mosses soft, and beds of flowers,
Crushing the kingcup into golden fire;
Whilst round us on the banks, the rabbits crop
The moist rich grass, or startled spring below,
Far bounding down the shaggy terrace' side.
Large seats of twisted wood, whose rude old arms,
Like those of Satyrs in Arcadia's prime,
Have circled many a gentle maiden's waist,
Are rooted here and there along the path,
Commanding all the distant hills and moors.
Soft as a spirit's breath, the summer wind
Low murmuring 'mongst the trees, makes music sweet,
And various as the leaves thro' which it goes.
Now surging like the mellowed roar of waves
On the sea-beach at even.—in the birch;
Now fuller sounding, like an organ's swell,
Thro' all the grand dark foliage of the oak.
And hark! how merrily in yonder copse
The blackbird's song makes all the woodland ring;
Whilst at our feet the sunny shadows flash,
And o'er us flames the vaulted dome of heaven.

" Tread lightly o'er the earth—and speak no word
Till the Great Spirit doth unloose your tongues.
For where those yew trees nod their funeral plumes
Upon the highest platform of the hill,
Lies gentle Robin Hood; his mighty heart
All muffled up in dust, and his bright eyes
Quenched in eternal darkness.   Never more,
Shall the woods echo to his bugle horn,
Or his unerring arrow strike the deer
Swift flying, till it bites the bloody grass.
Clean gone for ever all his merry band,
Who erst in gaberdines of green and gold,

Waylaid rich abbots in the Watlyne-street,
And broke their staves upon the Sheriff's men.
Broad-humoured Scathelock, and envious Much,
Will Stutely of the quarterstaff, and Tuck
The jolly friar, who liked more wine than prayer;
And all the hundred archers, vanished quite.
And she whom Robin loved, Maid Marian,
Light as a fawn, and beautiful as night,
When streams her starry hair along the heavens,
Rests like a lily, in the wild wood laid
Amongst the moss and violets.   Allen Dale,
The gentle harper, who was crossed in love,
Lies silent as the rest, his grave unknown.
And Little John, the master's favourite man,
Stiff in his giant bones at Hathersedge,
Sleeps on till doom, amongst the Derby hills.
So here the Head of this broad history,——
Who from his native hills in Loxley chace,
With Simon Montford fought at Evesham,
For the great Charter of the people's rights,
In unsuccessful battle, and became
A wild wood rover, rather than abide
The whips and arrows of a tyrant's power,——
Lies prisoned in black rails, his epitaph
Proclaiming all his woodland gifts and deeds.

" How lone and silent is the hallowed spot
O'ergrown with fringed ferns and mosses dank.
The tall dark pines in solemn threnody
Wail o'er his tomb—as o'er a wood-god dead,
And not a sound disturbs the deep repose,
Which like a slumbering spirit broods around.
Alas, poor Robin ! thou art dead and gone !
And We, who slept within the fiery womb
Of night and darkness, waiting to be born
When thou went down to silence in the grave,
Are here at last, to die and sink like thee
Again into the chambers of the dark.
So rise and vanish all the ghosts of men.

Away ! away ! we will no longer dwell,
On such a theme, in such a holiday;

For I and ye, companions of my walk,
Are strong in life and limb, and feel the blood
Like generous wine rush drunken thro' our veins.
O life! O glorious life! O world!
With thy great beauty sailing thro' the deeps,
Mid starry isles, and sunny continents
In the blue, lone, immensities of heaven,
I love you with a heart so full of joy,
That out it bursts over the happy hours
Like a far-circling all-embracing sea.
Life may be sleep—the soul's disease!
And death the true condition of a man.
But neither Plato, nor the mystic bards
—Great friends and well-beloved tho' they be—
Shall cheat me of my heritage on earth,
For I have no remembrance when the world
Looked otherwise than now it does to me;
Only, when I was very young, there seemed
To be an alien glory over all things.
And the great shadows of the ancient trees,
The supernatural shapes o'th' clouds,
The sun and moon and holy night of stars,
Flowed with a more divine significance
Into the windows of my soul, as if
They would recall the long-lost consciousness
Of a primeval fellowship with them.
So come away.   The past may not return.
Joy goes with youth, and wisdom slow with years;
The present moment is eternity.

    "Down thro' the trees to where yon rustic gate
Reveals the prospect of the park beyond,
We, from the outlaw's grave, will wend our way.
Lift up the iron latch.   I long to bound
Like those wild deer across the velvet sward.
Quick! for the sunshine lyeth all around,
And yonder, where the nunnery ruins stand,
I see our merry company advance.
Hark! to their trumpets and uproarious shouts,
And now away to meet them.

                    " Old and grey,
With narrow windows facing the dark woods,

The massy buildings of the nunnery stand.
Before them, on the slopings of the hill,
Huge groups of lofty trees—beneath whose shade
The hooded sisters of the convent walked
In dim old centuries, lying far behind—
Reflect their giant shadows in the brook,
Which with its music-voice flows on below.
The hospital, and dormit'ry, and barns ;
The long dark hall—whose iron window bars
Admit the straggling light thro' loops of stone ;
The old lodge chamber, where with treacherous skill,
To please fierce Roger Doncaster, 'tis said,
The Leech let out the life blood from the heart
Of the old outlaw, who had claimed his aid,
Sick lying at the posterns of the gate—
With all their ruined memories are here ;
And that low window saw the arrow shot
Which fell upon the place that marks his grave.

" Beyond the lodge, enclosed in mould'ring walls,
The convent garden lies.   The old oak door
Dropping with worms upon its crazy hinge,
Admits you stooping.   It is just the place
One would have thought to find in an old land
Long since deserted of all living men,
And given up to bats and dreary owls,
And lizards sleeping on the sunny walls.
Thick nettles choke the earth ; and hemlocks rank,
And strange, wild herbs, medicinal are there ;
With scents of rotting leaves and hyssop flowers.
The fruit trees bear the scars of fruitless age;
Their trunks all botched and knotted ; with grey moss,
And lichens cleaving to the hoary bark.
Their sapless branches bear no leaf or bloom,
But, bent and twisted, rot and fall to earth.
. Nature, well pleased with their old services,
Seems to reward them with a slow decay,
Protected from the violence of storms,
And pensioned on the bounty of the sun.

" Beyond the garden sleep the convent dead,
Promiscuous mingled with their mother earth.

The long, dark grass doth cover them ; and trees
Wave all their friendly shadows to and fro
Over the silent graves ; but not a stone
Is left to tell whose daughters rest below.
Alas ! sweet spouses of the Risen Lord,
Where now are all your chaunts and vesper hymns,
Which in the twilight chancels and the quire,
Amongst the sculptured effigies of saints,
Ye, in the chapel, sang at eventide ?
No more in lonely cell, your pallid cheeks
Shall glimmer in the broken light of stars,
Streaming thro' iron lattices ; no more
In holy reverence shall ye bow your heads
Before the Golden Image on the wall.
The night hath passed, and night again is here,
And many watchers wait to see the dawn.

    " Two tombs alone of all the monuments,
Which pious hands erected to the dead,
Within these sacred precincts, now remain.
One holds Elizabeth de Stainton's dust,
First abbess of the convent, now the last ;
Who with her sister here was laid to rest
Under the grassy turf and greenwood's shade.
But sacred evermore it is to me
This old religion, which nine hundred years,
Our English fathers lived in and died.
I love the large deep thoughts, the living fire
Which blossomed in the books and plastic work,
The paintings and the music of our sires.
And most of all the mighty architects,
Who, in the lack of words to represent
The vast creations of the labouring soul,
Built epic poems in immortal stone."

The Rector expressed himself on behalf of the company well pleased with the Maiden's performance, and I could see the eyes of the good Quaker light up with true pleasure and affection, as she sat down again beside him.

"I think," he said, "we cannot do better than spend the rest of this beautiful day where we are, in learning all we can about the Forest, and in listening to our musical friends. We can find beds at Ollerton, and Edwinstowe, I have no doubt; and to-morrow we will visit the scenes which we have heard, and may still hear, described to day."

The ladies were well pleased with this proposition, and as the Rector gave his approval, the matter was settled. And now continued our friend the Quaker, I have a real treat to offer you myself. It is a sketch of Harvest-Time in Sherwood Forest, by Christopher Thompson, and as I am the only farmer amongst you, I suppose I have most right to read about my occupation. Without more ado then I will begin."

HARVEST TIME.

"What a glorious morning! The golden-eyed sun is scattering the pearly dews of night, and filling the air with life-invigorating fragrance. The troop of sturdy-limbed mowers are casting aside their upper garments with a coolness which bespeaks their devotion to their task : already the sound of their tinkling scythes rings musically through the valley. The horny barley, that but a week ago was bristling its spiky head up heaven-ward, is now bowed down before the swathe-laying scythe. Upon the hill the shearers are gathered for their work : how their bright sickles glance back the sun's rays as the reapers bring them to bear upon the standing corn ! See yon little ruddy-faced boy; this is his first essay in the harvest-field : he is trying his hand at a withe to bind up the corn. His needy parents have taken him from the parish school to earn a few pence per day, for children must eat; and they have been looking long and anxiously for this season of harvest, hoping to repair the wreck which want of employment has made in their humble circle. The boy seems glad of this respite from school : how he bounds over the stubble like a fawn over the fern clad brooks ; and little wots he that long before sundown he will trail his now supple limbs right wearily along the new-shorn lands. All ages and both sexes seem eager for the toil : what a throng of them are there—home for once must be deserted—stalwart men, merry wives, jocund lads, and laughing maidens ; and under the shade of a bowering alder tree the careful mother has cradled her youngster with pillows and a store of old coats ; a sister, but twelve months older, is weaving him toys of yellow straws, and wreathing his young brows with bindweed, and despite the injunction not to leave her infant charge for one moment, she nevertheless bids him good speed until she shall return with blackberries from the hedgerows.

"Meantime the reapers 'lay to it,' and the corn rustles and falls before their sinewy frames: the day advances until 'drinking time,' and then, seeking the shade of some broad tree, the large basket is unpacked, the luncheon is handed round, and the iron-bound flacket is made to yield its brown beverage to the polished horn, and for the nonce the pain of labour is forgotten. The feast is over, and the leader sends round the cheerful cry of ' Now, my lads and bonny lasses, again to our work;' and so the day wears on. It is indeed a harvest day—intensely hot; the sky is grey with the palpitating vapour, and but one long silky cloud trails lazily across the arch of heaven : not a breath shakes the palmated leaves of those tall ash trees that hang over Maun's rush-fringed banks. The plaintive coo of the ringdove comes softy over Birkland's hays : the sheep press their fleecy carcases closely to the earth, and seem to wish they could bury themselves in the cool soil, and so escape from the myriad hosts of teasing flies ; how closely the stray ones from the flock creep around the mossy bole of that old thorn. If the traditions are to be believed in, what a story of olden time that patriarchal throne could tell ! It is the ' King's Stand Bush.' Upon that very spot, we are told, the kings of olden time were wont to gather for the regal sport of hunting the antlered deer through ' Shirewood's merrie glades.'

" And if the time-writhed arms of that old bush are no longer stretched forth to hold the bridles of the King's horses, or bear the green tunic of a royal huntsman, it still offers shade and shelter to a community—subjects they may be of Queen Victoria's—who sigh not for the purple or care for fine linen, who, subjects or not, are each of them kings in their turn. Their golden rule is ' love everybody and care for nobody.' Their right is might ; their palace court is the lane and the green wood ; their hall is well ventilated and very airy ; no sanitary commissioner need apply ; their ceiling is the sky overhead ; their carpet the emerald turf ; they fare sumptuously at all times ; and as for game, their gin is sure as was ever Norman's arrow, and their relish as good as the best of the Conqueror's village-razers, who are said to have burnt up whole villages to make room for their game preserves. There may be difference in matters of taste ; but if there is not as much variety—aye, and beauty too—in the picturesque attire of yonder camp of gipsies as you can find in an hour's lounge in Bond-street, my taste is vitiated.

" Mark yonder king as he turns down the lane—his brawny limbs, nut-tinted face, and flowing dress ; and his brunette, too, with eyes sloe black and raven hair, her red cloak and many tinted scarf ; their equipage, and stud of panniered donkeys. See ! seated in a huge basket, palanquined upon the donkey's back, is a young

ling; but, young as he is, he thinks the art of self-
defence when pugilistically applied may one day be
needed, so he is trying his initiatory craft; he doubles
his tiny fist and twirls his arms at me, as much as to
say, 'Stop, sir, while I am old enough!' They have
pitched their tent within bow-shot of the 'King's Stand;'
they have kindled their fire, and they will discuss their
dainties as freely as ever Robin Hood himself dispatch-
ed a red deer's haunch, or held in trust the purse of a
rich bishop. But the harvest time wears on; the sun
has sunk below the horizon, and is curtained by numberless clouds of roseate hue. With tired limbs the
reapers have sought their humble beds. Some of them,
poor souls, are huddled together in a neighbouring
barn; their mattress the straw lair; and their bed,
bedding, counterpane and all, an old sack, which the
charity of their employer has supplied: into this they
have crept in a state of nudity, and in it they hope to
repose as soundly as they did in their turf cabin across
the channel. Poor fellows! they may be the 'finest
peasantry' upon the earth. They can, probably, spare
a few minutes to contrast their furnitureless bed room
with the illuminated shows of their 'own little island.'
But all who are employed in the harvest operations
cannot go to rest with the sun. No, the rumble of
harvest wains rolls through the valleys like the sound
of distant thunder; and often until midnight the
driver's loud whistle, or his inharmonious measure of
'I heard a jolly sailor boy a singing'—'whop'—'haave
again, come hither'—'Captain, ah !' is heard again until
morning's dawn makes signal for the rest, if but for an
hour or two.

    "But the Sabbath yields to the field labourers soft
repose. Thank God for the Sabbath, for one day apart
from care-worrying toil ! Who can describe the sere-
nity of a Sabbath in the country ! Nor sound of sickle,
scythe, or wain, clacking mill, or clanging smith, breaks
the holy silence of a country Sabbath. The landscape
seems bathed in a sacred dreaminess, and the birds sing

more sweetly on that heaven-born day of rest. From
the quiet village, lone hamlet, and from every sylvan
nook, the peasant sons and daughters hie them to the
church, to list to God's revealed word, to pour forth
their souls in gratitude for those holy Sabbaths which
were given for them—that they can fearlessly travel
those footpaths to Heaven—that they can enter the
wide thrown portals of mercy, and enjoy those glimpses
of eternity, those foretastes of Paradise !

Morning again awakens the plodding husbandman,
and long before the sun has drank up the dews of night,
the 'cleared' corn fields are covered over with happy
children, who have sallied out to gather up the scattered ears that have escaped from the swathe-rake;
and in these days of union workhouses and ill fare,
happy are they who can eke out a scanty meal by glean-
ing up a few remnant ears of corn. And what of that
once celebrated feast the Harvest Home and supper, so
graphically sung by Bloomfield, where

> ' Once a year distinction lowers its crest ;
> The master, servant, and the merry guest,
> Are equal all.'

Are they to be banished from our rural records? How
seldom, now-a-days, 'distinction' honours this feast,
hallowed from the time of the Pharaohs to the nineteenth century. But the peasantry are superabundant
—the peasant is no longer his 'country's pride.' Man,
created in God's image, can be purchased at less cost
than animals; and we seldom hear of ' master, servant,
and merry guest,' sitting down together in the barn or
hall, and together rejoicing that the 'Feast of the
Harvest,' the 'first fruits,' are safely garnered. Poor
Clare was prophetic when he first sung of these rural
holidays :—

> ' Pride grows above simplicity,
>   And spurns them from her haughty mind;   .

And soon the poet's song will be
The only refuge they can find.'

Are then these soul-refreshing, simple feasts, to live
only in the poet's song? Is Mammon-worship hence-
forth to blunt the head of those who 'once a year'
made merry with all around them? Is the humble
peasant to brood over the debasing thought, that, now
despised, he is a mere 'hewer of wood and drawer of
water?' Is the song of the corn-reaper no more to
echo through our valleys and uplands? Forbid it,
Humanity! Let the reaper's chant live on; let us
hear again

'The last cart! the last cart!
Our maister's gotten his harvest home,
Well shorn,
Good corn;
A jack of brown ale for our own!'

"It is a mere rugged utility that cannot see beyond
the present. The pleasure of a harvest feast does not
finish with the beef and beer that is provided for it.—
No; throughout the year—at plough tail, in the
barn, the fold, the meadow—wherever labour called
him—the recollection of harvest-home was in the farm
worker; and when seated on his cottage hearth, by the
blazing faggot, on long winter nights, his careful dame
darning the hose in the nooking, his young ones
climbing his knees, he would crack his fingers and
sing—

'In harvest time, harvest folk, servant, and all,
Should make altogether good cheer in the hall;
And fill out the black bowl, so blithe, to their song,
And let them be merry all harvest time long.'"

When our friend the Quaker, had finished
reading this beautiful sketch, he said,

"If Christopher were not present, I could find it in my heart to praise him for the pictorial manner of his writing; and I should do so as sincerely, as I now thank him for the pleasure I have received in reading it." And the gracefulness of the compliment was acknowledged by the author with a silent smile; whilst his eyes kindled, and his cheeks glowed with animation and joy.

The Mater was particularly pleased with the sketch; and Miss M—— thought it would be delightful to turn gleaner in such hale and merry company—if it were only for the pleasure of forming a part of so picturesque a group, in the landscape."

"Ah! ah!" said the beautiful Governess, "but you would need the artist to paint your fairy-form in the corn-fields, my dear young lady, or the landscape would care very little about you. It is the eye that makes the picture. Persons are prosaic enough; and for that matter, so is Nature too; unless we can bring a cultivated spirit in the midst of her woods and streams, and so transform them into glory and beauty."

"One would think," interrupted the Rector, "that you had been reading 'Plato' my fair friend, to hear you discourse so learnedly upon this mystic subject; or 'Schiller's Æsthetic Letters,' perhaps; or January Searle's unfathomable lectures upon 'The Awakening.'"

"Stop," cried I, "if you please, Aristophanes!

and don't exhibit me that way to your audience!
for I am no Socrates,—nor half so good and wise
a man—but quite a 'fathomable' fellow; and
what I say in those 'Awakening' papers, is as
clear as the eyes of the 'Princes,' if not so deep.
Abuse 'Plato,' and 'Schiller' if you like, for
they can afford it—and what is more they are
dead and can't hear you; whereas, I am alive
and sensitive; caring, however, in reality, quite
as little what you say about me,—although for
different reasons,—as they do.   And whilst you
are reconciling the paradox, I will venture to
say that our sweet friend never read any of the
books you allude to, but discovered the 'mystic'
secret, as you call it, at the bottom of her own
pure and cultivated nature."

"You have just hit it, January!" said she,
looking at me with her large, bright eyes, and
smiling like a sunbeam;—"that is, so far as the
discovery is concerned," she added, with a slight
blush; "and what is more, Pater, you know it
is true."

"Certainly I do," replied the Rector, "and
that is the reason why I thought of Plato, when
you uttered it.   And now let us uncork another
bottle of Champagne; and perhaps your Royal
Highness, (addressing the Princess) will con-
descend to pass the Burgundy to that surly
January."

"Thank you," quoth I, "that is the best way

I

to end difference amongst friends.   And, by the by, that reminds me of a glee of mine set to music by one of my Halifax friends, which is well known to our musicians here.   Suppose we have it."

"Certainly! let us have the glee," said the Princess; and the Quaker and his little daughter joined their entreaties to hers in this matter, and so the glee was sung.

GLEE.

" Drink ! comrade, drink !
Why should we be sad ?
In the red wine sink,
All thoughts that are not glad.
There is enough of folly
'Twixt friends and foes.
Let us two be jolly;
Away with melancholy !
Time swiftly comes and goes."

Every body praised the music, which is arranged for four voices, and the Mater desired to know who composed it.

"As for that," said I, " he is a queer, incomprehensible fellow; full of dry humour, and as you will readily suppose, of music also.   He is a good player on the Piano-forte; is well acquainted with our poetic literature; reads German; and always carries a copy of my favourite Novalis in his pocket.   To crown his excellent good qualities, he is a member of the ' Church of Christ,' and a smoker. He is besides, an accomplished and pleasant companion; and I wish he and my friend Tom were with us just now."

"Tom?" inquired the Rector, "who is Tom, January? That is a friend I have not heard of yet, although I thought I knew everybody that you knew."

"True, Llandamman!" I replied, "you have not heard of him yet; but he is a fine fellow, I assure you; and I hope to introduce you to him before the Summer is over. What would your Royal Highness say, if a man measuring six feet, two inches of perpendicular flesh, of excellent proportions, and a face much handsomer (I beg your pardon, gentlemen,) than any I see here, were to make his appearance at your royal court, and ask the honour of attaching himself to your train and person? Well, just such a man is my friend Tom. He was of age only a few weeks back; and after studying hard at home, and mastering the German language and mathematics, he is about to start for Hesse-Cassel, where he means to spend three or four years, and will finish his studies in Paris. He is a generous, warm-hearted fellow, but for the most part silent and reserved in company, especially if there be anything to learn. He is a musician likewise; and when I go to see him, we always have a happy time; and discuss subjects, of serious import, which I am sorry to say, are not very popular in mixed companies. You would all love Tom, however, if you knew him, for he has a most affectionate nature, although he does not often show it in words. I assure you I expect great things from him; and am indebted to Thomas Carlyle for making me acquainted with him."

"If he is such a person as you describe him," said the Princess, looking archly upon the beautiful maidens around her, "I will advise you not to introduce him here, lest the ladies of my train should quarrel about him."

"No fear of that," interrupted the Rector, "so bring him as soon as you like; and in the meanwhile, we will call upon the Mater, to tell us what she has been reading about these last few minutes."

"Oh!" said she, "it is a little poem called the '*Forest Sunset*,' and if you will listen, I will read it aloud."

"Do so," said the Rector, "for it will suit the time and the place admirably well." Whereupon the good Mater read the poem.

THE FOREST SUNSET.

"The sun is setting; down the glade
  I see his brow of fire;
The forest-trees on tip-toe stand
  To see their god expire,
And the night winds sweep their trembling lyre.

" The skies are bathed with rosy light ;
    His head rests on a cloud.
 ' O ! leave us not,' the green leaves say ;
    But he lies in his shroud,
And the old, old oaks they sough aloud.

" The purple-hooded, sombre West,
    Has laid his red corpse out ;
And with him sinking down the heavens,
    Her curtain draws about,
And muffled shadows follow in their route.

" O ! aged Oaks, all black and bare,
    I pray ye, groan not so.
 O ! Birches, with dishevelled hair
    And voices weeping low,
Why do your eyes with tear-drops overflow ?

" He is not dead ! he does but sleep !
    He'll come again to you.
The night is here !   Come kiss her cheek,
    The starlight rushes through
The lattice-work of heaven to love you too.

" Lift up your heads ! the sweet young moon
    Is dancing o'er the grass :
Her smiles drop on you soft as snow ;
    Ye will not let her pass
Without one welcome, answering smile ? alas !

" Ah no ! dear Forest Hearts, rejoice !"—
    The bold Oaks shout amain ;—
The Birches weep no more, but wave
    Their arms without a stain,
And winds and woods are merry once again.

Evening had now come on ; stolen a march
of us, as the soldiers say ; and although it was

I 3

still light and clear as noon, yet it was a soft
and mellow light; the trees facing the west
were tinged with gold, and their dark and
beautiful shadows fell over the cool forest-
glades; and the birds were singing their evening
hymns to the praise and glory of God.

"It was on such a lovely evening as this," said
Christopher, "that I and Charles Rees Pemberton, 'the Wanderer,' as he called himself,
sat down under the shade of this venerable oak,
the first and only time that I saw him. He
came all the way from London, on foot, to spend
one day in the Forest, and very happy we were.
He was the most fascinating man I ever beheld.
You all know him, I dare say, by repute; but
if you never saw him you can have no idea what
I mean by calling him fascinating. He stole into
the deepest recesses of one's heart, like the
gentle sunshine; and his words were like love
itself. He was, however, a lonely and sorrowful man; but his large heart yearned to do good
to all living things. He gained his livelihood
by lecturing on Shakspere; and competent
judges have pronounced his lectures superior to
anything delivered in England, on the same
subject, before or since. His life was a singu-
larly interesting one, and he has embodied the
chief incidents of it in the '*Pelverjuice Papers*,'
which are published in his Remains, under the
editorship of John Fowler, of Sheffield. He
literally worshipped Shakspere, and once asked

a bookseller, who could not furnish him with a copy of the great master, 'whether he was not afraid his house would tumble over his ears?' He was impulsive in all he did; and his spirit was too fiery for reflection. Hence he was deeply loved, and deeply hated. For he was not a conventional man; and liked to say and do what he pleased. His face was intellectual, earnest, even to painfulness, and once seen could never be forgotten. He wore a tunic, and a leathern girdle around his waist; and you may see him, as he really was, in the Portrait, attached to his 'Remains.' His Sheffield friends, during the illness which carried him off, enabled him to visit Egypt, in the forlorn hope, that the climate might restore him. His letters from the Pyramids are highly interesting and characteristic. Poor Ebenezer Elliott loved him much, and when he died wrote these fine lines to his memory :—

"'POOR CHARLES.

" 'Shun'd by the rich, the vain, the dull,
    Truth's all-forgiving son,
The gentlest of the beautiful
    His painful course hath run ;
Content to live, to die resign'd ;
    In meekness, proud of wishes kind,
And duties nobly done.

" 'A god-like child hath left the earth,
    In Heaven a child is born ;

Cold world ! thou could'st not know his worth,
  And well he earned thy scorn :
For he believed that all may be,
  What martyrs are in spite of thee—
Nor wear thy crown of thorn..

" ' Smiling he wreathed it round his brain,
  And dared what martyrs dare ;
For God, who wastes nor joy nor pain,
  Had " armed his soul to bear,"
But vain his hope to find below,
That peace which Heaven alone can know ;
  He died—to seek it there.'

"I have here," continued Christopher, " the result of his visit to Sherwood, and perhaps the Rector will favour us by reading it."

" With all my heart," said he ; " please to pass the volume over this way."

"A PEEP INTO SHERWOOD FOREST.

" At the little out-of-the-way, undisturbed village of Edwinstowe, you can see no indication—nor, without previously-acquired knowledge, would you guess, that you are within five minutes' walk of the most perfect specimen of antique forest—the most sequestered and distinctly charactered elf and fairy realm on earth. It is the last vestige of Sherwood's right to renown. It stands alone, as it has stood for the last thousand years ; as it stood centuries before graceless King John, and his graceless nobles and courtiers, hunted the deer under its umbrageous boughs; before Norman William grasped the Saxon homesteads, and desolated the hearths of a hundred yeomen, to gorge one of his bull-headed fellow-ruffians. By itself it stands, and is like

no other spot on which my eyes ever looked, or
my feet have ever trod. It is Birkland—a beautiful
land of beautiful riches—with, near it—adjoining it, a
noble neighbour, *Billhagh*, or *Bellihagh*—all of oaks,
which have seen ten generations come and pass away.
Among the birches, too, stand many of those tall, huge,
bulky, and venerable giants. But come, reader, let us
walk to this Birkland, through the short street, through
the village, throwing, as we go, a passing glance at the
church's old tower and queer spire; and wondering
inquisitively at the odd fancy which placed the eight
niches at the tower's top, and the spire's foot; wherein
formerly stood as many grey-coated, grey-nosed, and
grey-skinned stone saints; which, an opposing sect of
image-worshippers—deeming the elevation of these im-
pious or idolatrous, dismounted and demolished. A
few paces more, and Edwinstowe is behind you; here
the road branches off in a Y-fashion; that to the
left inclining more to a right angle with the street;
the right-hand road leads to Thoresby Park—the left is
the road to anywhere, or nowhere; for as your eye runs
along it, you perceive it grows turfy and green, being
little trodden, except by sheep and harness-wains.—
Take either of these roads, but proceed directly onwards. Just at the junction of the forks, the apex of
the angle, is a company of tall, graceful trees—firs, and
other gentlefolks, towering aloft, and very beautiful;
look well at them; take impressions of them strongly
—they are the portal spirits to something more grand,
august—sublime; perhaps they are octogenarians, or a
century old; yet they will appear like striplings—
infants—by the contrast to which you are approaching.
Walk down upon that smooth, sinking sweep of undu-
lation: how gracefully it bends! like the mighty,
magnificent curve in a vast and green Atlantic billow,
which by some omnipotent—some invisible hand, has
been suspended in its rolling, and fixed thus as we
see it.

"'Here let the billows stiffen and have rest!' said

the great voice, and it was so. A stone covered well is all that breaks the verdant, rootless, tuftless, weedless surface; an upholsterer would not have nailed his green baize or drugget more evenly on your parlour carpet, nor glued his billiard-table cloth more *wrinklelessly*—so lies the verdant carpet—this fixed curve of the sea—till the uprising, crowning crest of the billow, ruffled with gorse, with its millions of yellow blossoms, the ocean spray changed into bright and burning gold, which mingles its glory with the bending blue of Heaven. That is the barrier-ridge which completely conceals the universe beyond; and is it not a gorgeous barrier? It is so resplendent in its beauty, that your heart throbs in loving worship of it. Here pause at its foot, and drink in the joy which it pours forth abundantly; and having done so, look upwards to the ridge, and without pausing in your step, as you wind to the summit, do but mark how those hoary-headed giants march up, forward, upon, into your vision—and from the ridge bound down that gently-inclining slope. In twenty steps, the world is quite shut out; you are in a strange, solemn, and old universe. You have passed from time to eternity—no, you have leaped out of the present, back, a thousand years. Your dull lump of earth—your hundred and forty pounds avoirdupois, more or less, of clay, is at once exhaled, or has dropped off, away from your existence; you are become unweighable essence—etheriality. You are all air—a bird—a spirit; you feel that you could leap like a cricket, with less than a cricket's ponderosity; ankle-deep you are enclosed in elastic moss, from which you rebound with the lightness of cork, or a ball of caoutchouc. Do not yet look around you, nor above you; close your eyes, and you breathe bliss; you float—sail—fly; you are in Heaven. Not yet—the chirping of the jackdaws tells you this still is Earth; for it is not yet said that jackdaws go to Heaven. Still this is Heaven; and you love it all the better on finding that it teems with the creatures of Earth—living, breathing, voiced creatures—and their speech-chirping here is delicious harmony—glorious concord. Bound a few steps more; you must bound—leap; you are full charged with electric fluid, and cannot *walk*. Stop! lift up your head, and gaze and gasp in the overpowering inspiration—which penetrates limbs—heart—and soul, and holds you mute awhile.

" A magnificent temple—the ruined Palmyra of the Forest—roofed by the wide arch of heaven! beautifully grand, awful, solemn, and deeply—intensely affecting; while it bows you down in adoration, it fills your spirit with love. There is nothing dark—nothing fearful—nothing sad in your soul, while you gaze; you do love it; it wraps you in a sublimity of affection; you feel it is all your friend—your parent—your guardian; it blesses you, while you worship it; and you bless it for the blessings it bestows. You feel that it was not the pride of man, nor the mockery of a false religion, which reared this wondrous temple; that neither fraud nor oppression mingled in the design; nor has human vanity ever desecrated the place with monuments to its honour. Grey and hoary with antiquity, the massive columns, though scathed, and rent, and bruised, by a thousand storms, yet uplift themselves in stately dignity; or, like reverend sages, more reverend from the scathe of elements, stretching out their arms in counsel, or upwards in appeal to the Father of Creation; and they look so nobly calm—so gently majestic! Enchained for a time is every faculty, corporeal and intelligent, till wondering love grows bold—familiar; but in that boldness it is reverential still; like the confiding assurance of candid and unsophisticated youth, in the supervision of an ancient man, whose face age has not crimped with frowns—whose voice peevishness has not cracked into treble-pipes of scolding—whose mortal beauty and benignity have grown under Time's touch—whose authority is benevolence. In the familiarity is no insolence, no presumption, nor servile courting of old wisdom's condescension. It is the open spirit of a child to a parent. So, on the subsiding of the floods of emotion, mingling awe, and love, and reverence, you stand amid this age-worn magnificence, and look upon those antique oaks with a deep serene joy. Your eye courses the whole; then approach and examine, in detail, parts and particulars; and how many images arise from the survey! Fancy suggests an alteration and succession of comparisons, and each comparison gives instant birth to its appropriate feeling. You ring the changes on your sensations, yet all are pleasant ones.

"Listen—you cannot avoid thinking that these venerable sages are going to speak: would they would! What lessons they might teach, what important secrets divulge—they who have looked on the world for ten centuries, what think they of the social system! Of what politics are they? Tory, Whig, Radical? What! Radical to a certainty, genuine, staunch, honest Radicals, for they would have all mankind happy, at no declension, no party's suffering. What tales they might tell of fear and strife, of hypocrisy and war, of song and sport, of mirth and laughter. Mirth and laughter! aye, there have been jovial doings in this hall of ages. Were not Robin Hood and his merry men, all occasional denizens here? To be sure they were; this was the favourite retreat, and here it was they took their metempsychosis, from jovial men, to jolly oak trees. There is Little John;—yonder tall fellow, with his one bare arm thrown out as if he had just swung his good quarter-staff in sport only, and pitched it to his neighbour, Will Scarlet, whose hand is held forth to catch it. No metempsychosis of the staff is to be seen—it is gone the way of all staffs; unless it has transmigrated to one of those brown ferns which are lying asleep on couches of moss. Friar Tuck is centupled. His spirit became prolific as it passed from its clay tenement, into oaken frame-work, and multiplied itself. Look at his girth enormous, and the huge wens starting from every side of his bulky carcass. They are relics of hogsheads of Nottingham ale that he poured down his tun-dish into his gulfy reservoir — laughing in the thorough base between every draught; and every car-buncle, bursting into a mouth, to let the laugh abroad, retains its thick lips in expansion of merry grin. He has literally split his sides.   Hark, ye jovial and vene-rated Foresters, news for you—news, at which you may start into flesh and blood again !—there is as good ale in Nottingham now, as ever was brewed when you drew long bow at the king's deer, or eased a fat bishop of his ungodly gold. So come back; no, not you. There are now no deer to shoot; and the bishops are all *too poor.*   Flesh and blood could not bear it. And of what race are those grotesque, fantastic, semi-monstrous forms, which stand commingled among so much of the dignified, venerable, and jovial ? Some are huge ser-pents, which have twisted their vertebræ into disloca-tion. Some are hard-mailed, long-tailed, fierce dragons, that have writhed in fury and agony till their necks, legs, and tails, have become fixed and lignified from torture.   And if yonder be not a griffin's head, griffin never was.   Heraldic painter, or carver, after a night's riding by night-mare, could not cut or paint a truer one.—Look at his acute nose, open jaws, and pointed tongue, and the pricked-up fox-like ears, with an eye as distinct and full as ever was eye; though, if you examine closer, it is but a hole right through the top-most fragment of a tree, which has been carved and cut by tempests working in aid of time.   How fiery would that eye be, if the moon peeped through it ! Were it night now, my old nurse's gossip, of hob-goblins and fiery fiends, would be busy with me; and nothing but a griffin's head would my superstitious imagination allow it to be.   The region is full of fantasy.

" But turn your eye to the left, westward : what see you there ? Is it a sun burst upon a line, a sheet, a field of silver? or snowy haze of a dewy exhalation floating beneath a denser and darker canopy of clouds ?

K

neither.   What thus fixes your gaze in admiration are the thousands of white and glistening stems of graceful birch-trees—silent spirits of beauty—sylphs in meditation—dryad-damsels, assembled there to dream. Look at them, and wonder at their glory.   Are you not impelled, attracted by a hidden and indefinable sympathy towards them?   How you wish and long to mingle your being and every sense with that quiet, harmonious, and delicious solitude which wafts to you a wooing invitation.   Then away!   spring over the elastic carpets of richly-tinted mosses—dash through the yielding heather barriers—pause and stop to look on the bright red stems that bend to your pressure, entwine round your limbs, and flash their beauty up into your eyes.   You are stepping on, through and over the annual renovated growths of twenty centuries, or more ; and the prostrate brown ferns, which crackle beneath your feet, will, in a few weeks, send up from their earth-hidden roots, thousands of tall, curling, green younglings, to mingle with the purple blossoms of the heather—then may you riot and roll in a sea of perfume—leap, spring, bound along ; now in a delight which feels not the clog of animality.   You inhale the exhilarating gas in such copiousness, that veins and arteries are no longer the channels of blood—they are all air-cells and electric conductors : the bird above your head floats not more buoyantly than you bound and sail on this precious bossomed earth.   Wind your way down to that broad line of clearing, that avenue of enchantment ; it seems to have been intended for a carriage road, but, luckily, the projector either amending his taste, or growing sick of the novelty, no longer charmed with his first vague, unfostering impressions of beauty, has abandoned it again to the old possessors, turf, fern, and heather.   Here walk awhile, slowly it must be, for you are fascinated into hesitation, and pause at every step.   There, they are, grouped in magical beauty, silent loveliness !   amid each group, in serious pride of contemplation, of the gracious forms and spirits around him, stands a reverend oak, smiling serenely, serenely and benignantly smiling, while he contemplates—the sultan of the harem ! but they are not his slaves—they are as free as himself. Yes, there they are, fair young nymphs; their slender forms enveloped in white silk and silver; their smooth silvery limbs just moving, and their abundant, glorious, pendulous tresses, swinging in the light wind ; swaying gently to and fro, their rich heads, and drooping locks, which are moving to the sweet music ;—that immortal harmony, which cannot be heard in our 'muddy vestiture of decay.' The sky above bends down upon the scene to look and listen, and clips the whole in an embrace of joy. Your soul is heaving and swelling in the fulness of happiness, of enchantment as you gaze here. Your heart floods with a rushing tide of eloquence; but speech is too poor to bear it along; and voiceless, and tongueless it rolls within, bathing and imbuing every faculty of thought and feeling, with the omnipotence of love. If you can, cast your reflections back upon the world you have left, far, far behind you, search the stores of memory, and examine each fibre of sense which memory agitates. Is there any bad passion? Is there any corrosion, any harshness; stirs there one breath of ill will to any human being? Is not all your soul steeped in benevolence? Is there one tinge of reflection which is not of love to all God's creatures? No, no; all are good, all are beautiful: you are what you would have all things, a totality of peace. You are a Christian, then ; you are adoring Heaven! Keep the instructions which these contemplations give you in your heart; store them there, and let them guide your practice when you mingle with the world.

"Twenty times have you been drawn towards the many embowered paths which intersect the body of the forest, each arched over, and diminishing to a point of light, or completely closed in, by the meeting branches; and you feel in anticipation the serene hush of the retreats to which they invite you; the repose from the tremour, the overcharged and overbubbling fountains of joyous and rapturous excitement. You long to enter and throw yourself at length on the couchy moss or fern, and quell the passionate sense into a tranquillity of satisfaction and retrospective thought. You have witnessed a beautiful drama, well got up and well performed, perhaps; one that has called up a succession of intense interests and enchaining sympathies; and you have gone home quietly, and through half the night coursed over each thought, emotion, and incident with calmer relish; thus fixing each more accurately and firmly on your mind's tablet. Just such a gratifying change and succession of pleasures are yours in gazing on those birches from the avenue, and then enwrapping yourself and thoughts, in one of these bowery mantles. So dash in at once, and *think* the pictures over. Come let us see what sort of a pic-nic we can make out here. This is a delectable spot for enjoying it; or take your selection from the hundreds of pretty canopied recesses and verdant alcoves, for a *salle a manger.* Or look there, there is a spot enclosed within a barrier of impenetrable gorse; if you like enclosures and barriers, which I do not, here you may sit or lie extended, screened in by a glorious curtain of green and gold.

Look, here is the entrance, somewhat intricate and winding, with room for one at a time to pass in; and space when you are there for a dozen or more, with swinging elbow room, as you assemble round the board? —No, round the smooth turf, which is covered with a snow white sheet of damask. Stay, who are, or are not to be of the party, and what the viands? These, sir, or madam, are matters to be well looked to, a little bungling will do great mischief, and utter freedom from arrangement will be the nicest order in the world, if you have set out wisely. I have seen so many of these things spoiled by nicety and decorum, that my philantrophy prompts a little advice to sylvan revellers. First, for the number of the party: if more than two,

do not stint at eight, ten, or a dozen, at least.   A dozen
will do, if you are sure they are of the right sort; and
this right sort does not include all who will answer
moodily "yes," to your question of "who will go?"
Be cautious that the desire to increase your number
does not coax you into an admission of doubtful ones,
or the pleasure of all must be sacrificed to that one's
inanity, dumbness, and deadness of soul.   For my own
single part, or whim, I should select children freely, as
fellows in the affair, because if they felt the inclination
to go mad with enjoyment, why mad would they show
themselves, and shout out of all 'proper behoving,'
and kick up their heels most unconventionally; all our
pleasures are doubled by the sympathy with others; so
let us have no propriety and decorum (those decoctions
of stupidity and cunning) here.

   "We will have those who can feel the beauties of
the place, and who, so feeling, will look, speak, and do,
all they can of all they feel—though it be to burst into
tears of rapturous hysteria—to scream with delight, or
to remain mute.   A majority of the gentle sex is de-
sirable.   If equally paired, you may be compelled to
tug and haul in couples, like grey-hounds.   For the
choice:—this is the nice point—the *experimentum
crusis*.   The right sort may be found from all ages,
from six to sixty:—(the fearful of rheumatics will not
do) but we have an instinctive aptness to the impression that personal prettiness, or, if you insist upon it,
beauty, is the store-house of all the lovelier qualities
of mind and heart; and it is so when rightly schooled;
but in the schooling lives and grows the mischief!
Generally, too generally—and this as much from the
contemptible foolery of the men, as from the narrowing,
conventional absurdity of their female instructors,
young ladies are taught into a mechanism of manner—
'springs to catch woodcocks'—to conceal, suppress,
crush all the natural and beautiful gushings of the
purest and most beautiful emotions, and to affect those
externals which are as much like the graces and beauties

of truth and delicacy, as a toad stool is like a violet or a primrose—a smile from one of which toad stools would curdle a whole sea of syllabub : one of such in this our projected party, would look Birkland into a huge birch-rod. Eschew all who were ever seen out of a dressing-room with hair *en papillotte ;* and all who would set forward on this jaunt, with hair and head tortured into the graces of a chizzle wig : there is no more poetry in such heads than in a dish of tripe; come, all who do come, with tresses that will freely unloose themselves from their braids; so that locks and ringlets may swing in companionship and sympathy with the thousands of tassels on the heads and brows of these Lady Birches. How glorious looks a young creature as she springs, light as an antelope, over the moss and through the heather, and darts in and out among the entertwining sprays, in the joyance of a heart that makes buoyant and elastic every limb and sinew; with tresses sportively floating, waving and fluttering in the wind ; now shadowing the light of her eyes, now parting aside to let forth the full and brilliant flash of the happy spirit within : making nature proud at beholding her child. Let every one be in woodland trim ; that is fit for a scramble through the branches and the gorse; all sylvan delight is alloyed, destroyed if there be any demand on your attention or care lest your dress should be disarranged or damaged. Against long tails, flounces and frills, netting and gimping, and furbellows, the Forest has declared ceaseless and persevering warfare : so let your outward man, or woman, boy or girl, be such as it will not affect your delicacy to see rendered somewhat more picturesque at the close, than it was at the commencement of the revel ; though indeed, there is little likelihood of fractures, if you have been wise in your equipment—dress so, that you can be altogether in the thorough don't *carishness* for scratches. A beaver hat is a villain in the woods; a shawl or veil, no less so. Sandals, too, are an abomination ; their strings make so many unloving alliances with underwood and roots so neat-fitting stringless shoes, or ankle-boots, with lace ends carefully, snugly tagged in, if you please, ladies !

"Well, the selection is made, the party is assembled; all of eyes that can see beauty, and hearts that can rejoice in it; of spirits so incorrupted that they will yield his or her own reeling, give and receive enjoyment and full scope to the expression of enjoyment, and each in what is an indispensable characteristic, will not pretend to enjoy where enjoyment is not. So march ye now in order,—no order at all,—into this calm realm of forest, grandeur, and glory. I'll tell you what such a party will do: first, assemble in a compact knot, (without designing, planning, such assemblage; and it would be a tedious wordy process to show you the *why* of this) as if to catch and communicate inspiration from all to all; it is to that, you so assemble, but you do not know what attracts you:—to hear the short ejaculations of surprise and subdued exclamations, murmurings, and breathings of pure rapture,—deep and holy is that rapture, and in that delicious variety of expression it shows itself! What next! Then you draw off by twos and threes for a while, till a more vivacious, exhilaraing, dancing delight courses rapidly through the nerves; and then, in as many directions as there are animated beings to take them, bound forward over moss, through glade and heather, in very exuberance of bliss. Nay, I should not be surprised if some ran up to the trees, and kissed them; nor should I regard such an *extravagance* as aught but the gushing that throbbed with the love of nature, which superior intelligence and perception of beauty, moral or physical, animate or inanimate, *does* awake, and does fan its pure sparks into an unsullied, forth-issuing flame. Your eye looks yonder on a fawn like creature, for agility; bounding along, now hidden, now glimpsingly seen through the dangling branches, or peering over some fern-brake or gorse-bush; there sits another on a grassy seat, lost in abstraction of meditation; as full of sweet poesy is her soul, as is the air with balmy freshness: there is one

stooping to examine with curious admiration the minia-
ture forest which her fancy has found in a moss tuft,
and wondering if these little scarlet-headed fugus-
sprouts, are not torches by which the beetles light up
their supper halls : there is another, pencilling on her
brain the elegant and picturesque trunks, slender arms,
whip-like branches, and delicate foliage of a group of
trees, and catching impressions of the moving lights
and shadows which play about them, telling herself
that she can make a good sketch from memory when
she reaches home, or that she will come again, and have
it from the life ;—another day's enjoyment laid up in
the store-house of her anticipation. Away, in distance,
mellowed into the sweetness of a sweet sound's echo,
now heard, now lost, a warbling voice is streaming out,
the spirit's cascade of joy; all is so happy, that the very
trees have a living sympathy with it, and participate in
breathing being.

But now call in the stragglers, call in the frolicksome,
unchain the enchanted, halloo to the warbler, break the
fixed muteness of the contemplative, and all gather in,
with one look, one set of thoughts;—here is our hall, our
tent, our refectory ; and here the viands. What? First
for seats and tables. The smooth green turf within the
enclosure of gorse, of which I aforetime spoke, for the
latter; and for seats, in ten minutes as many hands
have collected moss sufficient to furnish the hall with
more inviting sofas, and easy chairs, than ever were
conjured up by the luxurious ingenuity of a Hope or a
Beckford. Come, suspend your hats and bonnets to the
swinging branches ; the strings will flutter as so many
festival streamers; throw shawls and handkerchiefs
on, and among the gorses, yellow flowers, and heather ;
there's an eye gladdening commingling of colours ! Sit
or recline at your pleasure ;—room for either or for
all. Ours is the general, co-operative system,—each
assists the other ; we have neither masters nor servants,
but all are each, a regular levelling of ranks and ages ;
we do not exclude the little ones till the big ones are

accommodated, nor bid the juniors wait 'till their elders are served;' no, nothing of that have we among us. We have utterly abjured the fag system, now, and forever; we deny the right of the strong to oppress the weak, and we ever will deny it: we will walk and sit, eat, drink, talk, and breathe, in perfect equality of kindness. Our table is covered with damask, pure, clean, snow-white; remember, it must, it shall be so. Knives and forks spotless and speckless; remember this too; we will have no make-shifts of what we do bring in the way of viand furniture; if a plate or dish be cracked or chipped, in the carriage, away with it! over the barrier it goes; our drinking glasses are crystal, clearer than any mirror, or green, like the overhanging foliage, and sharply conical, tapering to their stems in the finest point. I have sound argument in advocacy of such shape; viz., it conveys the liquid in a smooth, unbubbling, unbroken streamlet, down upon the delicately fashioned grove, which your tongue makes to receive it, and so wafts it home; whereas your globular, or flat-based chaps, send it into your mouth, with a splash and a gullup. And for wines, we will have nothing but your gentle creatures; Hock, Moselle, Sauterne, and that family; no blustering Port, no bitter or burning Sherry; and eschew malt, as you would one of the toad-stools; Champagne is a mischief; it unscrews the pegs of the soul's fiddle, or cracks the strings;—produces first a crash, or a rant, and leaves nothing but discord and drowsiness; our selection keeps all in tune. Port, Sherry, Malt, Spirits, avaunt ye! we must not have such here; they will engender Englishism as you look on the trees,—a cutting or tearing them up, or a wish that they were your 'property,' or a calculation of how much money they would make. For viands, *do* be nice in these; avoid sandwiches, all fat, butter, grease; no mustard; bread as white as hound's tooth, and short and crisp as skill can make *it.* We will have a salad,—aye an English one,—a rustic—

no oil, no mixture of yellow butter with it; the right
countrified vinegar and sugar rectifier. Now eat,
drink, laugh, and be merry; and having cleared the
wreck, give thanks by listening to the twang and tink
of that guitar, and the song which it accompanies; or
if there be one in the ring who can read as if what
he (or she,) read, were an emanation of his own thoughts,
who can read as he would speak, tinging what he
reads with the colours, the varieties of modulation and
tone, to which the sentiments, scene, and incidents, and
character of the subject, would freely give birth to,
hear him or her. Such a one is too good a judge to
select a pastoral or woodland description; he knows
that all such things must be tame and insipid here, in
the presence of surrounding realities. Read those
matters when away from their realities, to rekindle the
enjoyment, to recreate the scene, and give a deeper impression to your memory. A ball or drama of incidents, developing character and emotions, is better
now; and mark how much more acutely and accurately
you will estimate motives, appreciate actions, sympa-
thize with feelings; how your indignation will rise at
fraud and oppression; how you will scorn and smile in
contempt at cunning paltriness; how you will sympa-
thize with beauty of heart; how readily acknowledge a
simple deed of affection, and how you will glow with a
new, and perhaps hitherto unknown delight, at the
triumph of good feeling and honesty struggling through
difficulty; you will weigh the deeds of warriors in the
scale with intellectual courage, and moral daring, and
the mind's independence, and hence find the warrior's
renown as a feather against them; you will see heroes
as a whirlwind, which raged out the desolation of millions, for the gratification of their own avarice, or their
own exaltation; your soul's voice shall be tuned in
rich harmony, and join the choir whose song is; 'the
world and its human creatures shall be happy; life is
not a vale of tears; it shall stream a river of joy.' Oh,
it is good to walk where Nature unfolds her beauty,

LEAVES FROM SHERWOOD FOREST. 167

amid her silentness, and you carry good back into the bustling world, from these occasional visits to her flowery and woodland domains.

"And now you are called homeward, but ere you leave Birkland, collect again to gaze, to drink in, the closing draughts of pleasure which the hospitable friend gives freely; and ere your foot is turned to leave it, you have each and all uttered a wish to revisit the scene, and have formed a scheme for accomplishing the wish; then, 'Bless you, Birkland! good bye, for the present; and remain for ever in your beauty!'

"What says your genuine practical man, as he calls himself, to all this? He professes to advocate utility; yet affects, and indeed, does despise, the utilitarian: the far reach of those views this man can no more compass in his thoughts than he can grasp between his fingers the winds of Heaven. This practical man feeds and fattens on the produce of larger minds, yet pities or scorns the fructifying spirit which supplies him with his health—his food—which opens to him the sources and the mines from which he gathers his harvest, and accumulates his worldly substance. What will he say? Why that all this is fantastic enthusiasm, visions, untenable Utopia. He wants 'something useful,' Is not this useful? 'No; what will it sell for? what can be made of it? what will it fetch in the market?' Possession—buying and selling, enclip all his heart of utility; and he despises the utilitarian, whose calculations are as to the sum of happiness which may be so diffused, that all may share. I had a rencontre with one of these practicals travelling from north to west. He was too 'polite' to laugh in my face, but no doubt I have been a good butt of merriment to him. He was 'all for utility:' could not find anything but barrenness on Sherwood Forest, and would be glad to see the plough producing something by being passed over the gorse, heather, and moss; he should like to see it all inclosed—somebody's property! Hah! 'Yielding a crop of wheat, grass, or oats.' Crop! inclosures for him, and exclusion too. The hundreds of poor cottagers whose cattle and sheep browse on the heather, and beautify the swelling elevations, slopes, and hollows, are no consideration in comparison with the gratification of some avaricious landholder's desire to grasp at more; whose extent of domain begets other feelings than a fury for a greater extent; and authorizes him in the covetous greediness of his grasp. No matter though the sandy, thin, and bony surface of soil, will never repay the expense of tillage—it is to secure *possession* of it, which is desired—some more thousands of acres to swell the sound of 'my property,' 'my estates,' and stare upon the moss which hangs in the hall to be gazed at, and envied by all comers.

"I am 'a cold and heartless' utilitarian—and have a faith in the progression of human improvement and in the perfectibility of man. There is genuine poetry in those woods—and on those moss and heather swells and dells. The richest mass of utilitarian treasures, those leaders to perfectibility, lies in the springs of poetry; springs of purest sources; and they stream along, aiding, nurturing, and encouraging all that is pure; peace within your own breast, and love to others. Poetry is feeling's truth—its language is truth feelingly uttered;—feelings are our soul's strength, the stays of our intellects. Utility! Is not happiness utility? 'Yes.' Then you store up utility, at no one's damage, by roaming Sherwood Forest, and going mad, if you choose, in the place in which I have been revelling. 'But it is not lasting—it is not tangible—you lose the feeling with the presence of the scene, or excitement.' Oh, not so; it has sunk into the deeps of your heart, and you can, whenever you will, as a miser can revisit and gloat over his hoards of gold, unlock the deeps with the key of your memory, and feed again and again upon your feeling; unlike the miser, you dispense your treasures freely—nor will repetition of the giving, and the repast diminish the stores, or render insipid the true relish, which you tasted in their first freshness."

As Christopher finished reading Pemberton's Sketch, the sun, which had for some time past hung over the distant forest like a lamp of fire, illuminating all the trees with his glory, gradually sank down into the chambers of the West, and resigned the world to the quiet keeping of the dim and dreamy twilight.

"How beautiful," said Miss M., "it would be to have a dance on the green-sward at this sweet and witching hour. What say you, dear Pater!—will you join us?"

"Certainly, my bonny darling!" answered the Rector, and, rising from his seat, he took the hand of the fair girl in his, and called upon us all to join them.

The ladies wanted no second invitation; but we men were in a quondary. The Quaker could not be expected to dance, although I knew that he loved to hear the tinkling feet of merry youth, and delighted to watch their graceful and melodious motions. Neither could giant Widdison take a part in these proceedings —for how could the maidens clip his waist?— and as for me, I never tried my foot at this work but once—(it was at Wisbeach, in the year 1838, I think, and I was handed from the gallery of the Infant-School there, by poor Louisa H., now dead, alas!—who insisted that I should be her partner in a country-dance) and no poor wretch ever cut a more sorry figure than I, upon that occasion. Fancy a cow in

the act of running; and you may then form
some idea of my unwieldy way of dancing. The
truth is I don't like the amusement—which to
me is no amusement, but torture—although I can
sit and look on others engaged in it, with real
pleasure.   Christopher and Trueman, however,
having no natural disqualifications, and no
antipathy to it, joined the circle with great
gusto; and a right merry dance they had of it.

We afterwards wandered through the glades
in the moonlight; and saw the stars shining
through the tree-tops as we passed along, whilst
the nightingales made us glad with their musical
and melancholy pipings.   And then how calm,
silent, and beautiful was the old Forest! and
how sweetly the evening wind sang amongst the
trembling leaves.   Every now and then a number of rabbits crossed our path, and as we passed
the glade leading to Bilhaugh, an owl flew from
the hollow of one of the oaks, and hooted, with
its loud " *Tu-whit! Tu-woo!*" along the dusky
forest aisles.   We returned to the village with
song and music in our train.   Unfortunately
there was no inn sufficiently large to entertain
us all at Edwinstowe, and we were obliged to
take up our quarters at Ollerton for the night.
So we bade farewell to our Forest friends, and
promised to visit them again next day, and in-
spect the various places of interest, in and around
Sherwood.

It was nine o'clock in the evening when we

arrived at Ollerton; and as we passed the river, we saw one or two fishermen whipping for trout; and the old Forest looked so grand and dark, that some of us were tempted to return to it. The Rector, however, thought we · had better spend a quiet hour in the inn; accordingly we acquiesced; and after the usual bustle and hurry, consequent upon an arrival so late at night, we were shown into a large and comfortable room, well lighted with wax candles; and here we conversed upon the events of the day, and drank a cup of sack to the memory of Robin Hood and Friar Tuck.

The ladies flung themselves upon the sofas; but our good friend, the Quaker, on seeing a piano in the room, called upon the "Princess" to play some song or overture, as a finish to the beauty and harmony of the day. She arose, therefore—her long black hair streaming over her neck and shoulders, with a sweet smile upon her face, and opening the instrument, sung the following song, composed by George Tweddell, called

"THE ENGLISH HEARTH.

"When Autumn's fruits are gather'd in,
  And trees and fields are bare;
When merry birds no more are heard
  To warble in the air;
When sweetest flowers have droop'd and died,
  And snow is on the ground,
How cheerful is an English hearth,
  With friends all seated round.

" Then is the time for festive mirth,
    Then is the time for glee ;
'Tis then the tales of by-gone days
    Give pleasure unto me ;
And when the wild storm howls without,
    With deep and hollow sound,
I love the cheerful English hearth
    With friends all seated round.

" And when those touching strains are sung,
    Writ by the bards of old,
How swift the evening seems to fly—
    Unfelt the piercing cold ;
What though the snow-flakes quickly fall,
    And icicles abound !
I have a cheerful English hearth
    For friends to sit around,

" Then fill each glass with nut-brown ale,
    And smoke the fragrant weed ;
Our English hearths we will protect
    In every hour of need :—
Come, let us drink one parting toast,
    Through Europe let it sound ;
It is—The cheerful English hearth,
    With friends all seated round !"

The ladies soon after retired to rest, and when they were gone, I rung the bell for tobacco and pipes, and we had a pleasant talk of it until midnight.

I threw open the window, and sat amongst the folds of the ample curtains, that I might "take mine ease at mine inn," and talk and smoke, and enjoy the moonlighted landscape which lay stretched before me.   I think Nature is more beautiful by night, even than by day.

At all events she is more mysterious and solemn; and I never enjoyed her loveliness more than upon this occasion. Every thing was still and calm around me, as I looked forth into the blue and starry heavens, and gazed over the meadows and woodlands. Occasionally, I heard the distant voices of children in the village, and once or twice the bark of some faithful house-dog broke upon my ear. Otherwise, no sound disturbed the silence of the landscape. My good friends, however, would not let me long enjoy my dreams, for they kept up such a running fire of conversation, and sent so many shots into my quarter, that I was at last obliged to "'bout ship," as the mariners say, and fairly engage them, broadside to broadside.

"If I remember rightly," said the Quaker, "William Howitt has written a description of the Forest, has he not?" "Yes," I replied, "and it is one of the best descriptions of Sherwood we have. I am very sorry Christopher had not a copy of Howitt's "Rural Life of England" with him to-day, that we might have read it."

"Well, never mind," said the Rector, who was a philosopher, and took every disappointment very coolly, "we will supply that loss to-morrow, and I heartily wish both William and his charming wife Mary could then be with us to enjoy the scenery, once more, which he has so well depicted in his books."

L

"Nothing would give me greater pleasure," I replied, "than such a reunion; for I long to see these beautiful people again, and I shall never forget the happy hours I have spent at their delightful home in Clapton."

"Then you know them personally?" asked the Quaker.

"Yes! such is my good fortune," I replied; "and I never met with more true and noble-hearted people."

"Pray, then," rejoined he, "give us some little sketch of their personal appearance and demeanour; for thou knowest they are, or were, of my cloth; and I am, moreover, much attached to them for their fine perception of the beautiful, and their deep love for moral truth and excellence."

"When I first saw them," I rejoined, "they were living at Upper Clapton; and I rode over from London by omnibus to see them.— The driver knew them as well as he knew his own horses, and set me down under the elm trees before their garden gate. I rang the bell, and was ushered into the hall, whilst the servant went to announce my name. I introduced myself as a friend of Spenser Hall, who at that time was in the height of his mesmeric career, and a guest of the Howitts. I was presently introduced into a large and lofty room, where I found a middle-aged man, almost bald, with a few white locks scattered over the sides and back of his head, seated by the fire (for it was winter time) along with a little boy about twelve years old. He rose to welcome me as I entered, and there was so much hearty hospitality in the reception that I was soon quite at home. This was William Howitt, and the little boy was one of his sons. In personal appearance, Howitt is the beau ideal of an English gentleman. He is about the middle height, rather stout, and has a fine, open, and manly countenance. His complexion is very fair, and his eyes are of a light grey colour, I believe, but am not quite sure of this. You cannot be mistaken however in his bland and genial look, and feel sure that you have met with a man who is at once kind, and true. The Phidian polish of his features, and the huge mass of brain which piles his forehead, bespeak the brilliancy and strength of his intellect; and his conversation well sustains the impression made by his appearance. He is blunt and straightforward in his speech, but not rudely so; and you see that this is the natural expression of an honest and manly heart. He apes none of the manners, and assumes none of the affectations which repel and disgust us in certain noted literary men; but he is simple and warm hearted, loves his friends, and is beloved by them. A genuine benevolence animates all his actions; and he delights to help struggling genius and worth into notice. He has lived too long in the world to take his opinion of any unknown writer's merits from that of other men; and wherever he finds talent, he honestly proclaims it, and sets it forth with a generous hand in his literary reviews. His "History of Priestcraft" will have prepared you to hear that he is a hater of oppression and cant; and I never heard him utter a bitter word, except against Priestly and Aristocratical fraud, and domination. I need not tell you that he is, in his religious views, a Quaker—so called; for although he has long since dropped the garb of his order, and released himself, I believe, from the communion of these excellent, but rather straight-laced people, (always excepting present company, friend Thomas,) yet he cleaves to the high faith which Fox taught, and believes in the influences and mystical revelations of the spirit. He need not be a Quaker, however, to believe this, for it is a doctrine as old as man, inculcated long before Plato, and revived in these times by German metaphysicians, and by our great dead poets, Wordsworth and Coleridge. Well, after having talked awhile upon various subjects, I asked if I could not speak to Spenser Hall, and was told that he was making mesmeric experiments in the drawing room, preparatory to a lecture he was to deliver in the evening, under Mr. Howitt's presidency. A few minutes afterwards, a lady entered the room, almost as silently as a sunbeam; and asked for some little article she wanted, in a whisper. She had just left Hall, and had brought the mesmeric atmosphere, and feelings with her, and this was the reason of her noiseless movements. Mr. Howitt introduced me to her as his wife, and I had the pleasure— and a real pleasure it was, I assure you,—to shake hands with this charming woman. She was dressed in black silk, and wore a handsome matronly cap. In her youth she must have been a very interesting, if not a beautiful woman. The expression of her face was shrewd and intelligent, and her eyes—which are dark and fine—literally looked one through. I had not time then, however, to get any true insight into her character; for she speedily left us, and returned to the drawing-room, where I was presently summoned. As I entered I saw Spenser Hall standing before a patient whom he had succeeded in sending into the mesmeric state, and from whom he elicited many singular mental phenomena. I will not trouble you to-night, however, with any detail of them, and will only add that I spent a very happy day with these excellent people. The whole family met together at the dinner table, and I was introduced to Miss Howitt, a very beautiful and intelligent girl, who has since devoted herself to art, and is rising rapidly, I hope, in her profession. I forget the number of Mr. Howitt's children, but they formed a goodly group around the table, which was plainly, but plentifully served. In the afternoon we had music and singing, and Mrs. H— related some of her German experiences, and gave sketches and related anecdotes of noted and literary people there. Several friends dropped in to tea from Town, and we spent a delightful evening. Mrs. Howitt is essentially a lady in her manners, breeding, and culture ; and her admirable qualities, both of mind and person, appeared to great advantage on this memorable evening. She was kind and affable to all, and it was beautiful to hear the music of her voice, when the conversation became animated."

"Thou may'st well remember the Howitt's, January," said the Quaker, " and now suppose we go to bed and dream about them."

"Certainly, if you are tired," said I ; and with that we departed.

Next morning we breakfasted by seven o'clock, and visited during the day, Rufford Abbey, Clipstone Castle, Cresswell Crags, and Markland Grips, Welbeck Hall, Thoresby Hall, Budby Forest, The Shambles Oak, and the most remarkable scenery in the Forest for several miles round.

At some future time I may relate the adventures of this second day's visit to Sherwood. All I can say about them now is, that John Trueman sang the two songs which I give below, as we stood together under the ruined walls of Clipstowe Castle, looking down upon the sweet little cottages in the village.

"THE MAIDEN AT HER SPINNING WHEEL.

" Round goes the wheel, the merry wheel,
    The sun shines bright and clear;
The flax is spinning on the reel,
    The lark is singing near.

" Up ! up ! he mounts to heaven away,
    The bird of lowly nest ;
Hark ! to his wildly gushing lay,
    The dew is on his breast.

" He meets the morning in the skies
    Upon his dappled wings.
It seems to rain down melodies,
    In the glad song he sings.

" Over the landscape green and brown,
    Bright golden shadows fall ;
But O ! the Lark's song cometh down
    More golden than them all.

" The Forest minstrels all are mute;
    No other sound is heard,
Save low wind breathings like a lute,
    With which the trees are stirred.

" He singeth yet a wilder strain
    As nearer heaven he soars ;
What visions float within his brain,
    That these fresh notes he pours ?

" Ah ! tiny bird, how deep a heart
    Within thy bosom dwells ;
Would thou its meaning could'st impart,
    And what thy flight impels."

"THE MINSTREL TO THE MAIDEN AT HER SPINNING WHEEL.

"The Nightingale singeth of love,
    As I am now singing of thee;
He hath a mate in the heaven above,
    As a lover thou hast in me.

" She died in the violet time,
    And left him alone in the Spring;
As I shall die e'er the Summer's prime
    If thou spurnest the love I bring.

" He seeth her eyes in the starry skies,
    As I see heaven in thine;
And his spirit rushes in music gushes
    To kiss thee as they shine.

" He cannot rest till he clasp her breast,
    Nor cease his wild love lorning;
And oh, my heart, it will break apart,
    If I clasp not thine this morning,"

"Bravo !" said the Quaker, when John had done singing, "that smells of the olden days of Romance and Chivalry ;" and so we passed on to Budby Forest.

FINIS.

STANDARD WORKS
SOLD BY
G. PHILIP & SON, LIVERPOOL,
And may be had of all Booksellers.

JOHNSON'S LIVES of the POETS, with Critical Observations on their Works, 2s. 6d.

ROBERTSON'S HISTORY of SCOTLAND, with an Appendix, containing Original Papers, 2s. 6d.

The COMPLETE WORKS of ROBERT BURNS, with an Account of his Life, and a Criticism on his Writings, by Dr. Currie, 2s. 6d.

ROBERTSON'S HISTORY of AMERICA, 2s. 6d.

SMITH'S WEALTH of NATIONS, 2s. 6d.

The ORATORS of FRANCE; including Mirabeau, Danton, Bonaparte, Foy, Garnier-Pages, Lafayette, Odillon Barrot, Lamartine, Guizot, Thiers, etc., 1s. 6d.

The CZAR, his COURT and PEOPLE; including a Tour in Norway and Sweden, by Maxwell, 1s. 6d.

CHAPTERS IN THE HISTORY OF A LIFE, by January Searle, 1s. 6d.

A VISIT to CONSTANTINOPLE and ATHENS, by the Rev. Walter Colton, 1s. 6d.

BURNS as a POET, and as a MAN; by Samuel Tyler, 1s. 6d.

REFORMS and REFORMERS of Great Britain and Ireland, 1s. 6d.

The PANORAMA of SCIENCE, or, Guide to Knowledge, by George Grant, 1s. 6d.

CHRISTMAS HOLIDAYS in ROME: by Dr. KIP, 1s.

The LIVING ORATORS of AMERCA, by E. L. Magoon, 1s. 6d.

LOITERINGS in EUROPE; or, Sketches of Travel in France, Belgium, Switzerland, Italy, Austria, Prussia, Great Britain and Ireland, by J. W. Corson, M.D. 1s. 6d.

CLARKE'S TRAVELS in Russia, Tartary and Turkey, illustrated with a fine steel engraving, 2s.

WANDERINGS of a PILGRIM, in the Shadow of Mont Blanc and the Jungfrau Alp, by Dr. Cheever, 1s. 6d.

BUCHAN'S DOMESTIC MEDICINE, 1s. 6d.

The LIFE of SIR WALTER SCOTT, Bart., 1s. 6d.

The LIFE of WALLACE, the SCOTTISH HERO, 1s. 6d.

BIOGRAPHICAL SKETCHES of LOUIS NAPOLEON BONAPARTE, First President of France, 1s. 6d.

THE HISTORY of the UNITED STATES of AMERICA, from their first settlement, 2s.

MECHANIC'S OWN BOOK, embracing the portion of Chemistry applicable to the Mechanic Arts, with abstracts of Electricity, Galvanism, Magnetism, Pneumatics, Optics, Astronomy, and Mechanical Philosophy, by James Pilkington, 1s. 6d.

KINGS AND QUEENS; or, Life in the Palace: consisting of Historical Sketches of Josephine and Maria Louisa, Louis Phillppe, Ferdinand of Austria, Nicholas, Isabella II., Leopold, and Victoria, by John S. C. Abbott.

The HISTORY of USEFUL INVENTIONS, 1s. 6d.

PROVERBS FOR THE PEOPLE ; or, Illustrations of Practical Godliness drawn from the Book of Wisdom, by E. L. Magoon, 1s. 6d.

D'AUBIGNE and his Writings, 1s. 6d.

RURAL LETTERS, and other Records of Thought at Leisure, by N. Parker Willis, 1s. 6d.

A TOUR through ARMENIA, PERSIA, and MESOPO- TAMIA, by H. Southgate, 1s. 6d.

OBSERVATIONS in EUROPE, principally in FRANCE and GREAT BRITAIN, by John P. Durbin, D.D., 1s. 6d.

TRAVELS in MEXICO, during the years 1843 and 1844, including a description of California, the principal Cities and mining Districts of that Republic, the Oregon Territory, etc., etc., 1s. 6d.

The LIFE of ROBERT BRUCE, the Liberator of Scotland, by George Grant, 1s. 6d.

POPULAR GEOGRAPHY ; or, A General Description of the Five Great Divisions of the Globe, by do. 1s. 6d.

BRYDONE'S TRAVELS in SICILY and MALTA, 1s. 6d.

SIGHTS in the GOLD REGIONS, and SCENES by the WAY, 1s. 6d.

A HISTORY of LONDON from the earliest period to the present time : comprising the Rise and Pro- gress of the Metropolis, by do., 1s. 6d.

TRAVELS in ITALY, the ALPS, and the Rhine, by J. T. Headley, 1s. 6d.

Sold by G. Philip & Son, Liverpool.

ELEGANT GILT VOLUMES,

At One Shilling Each.

THE GARLAND OF EVERGREENS, AN OFFER-
ING OF FRIENDSHIP.

FORGET ME NOT, a Token of Love and Friendship.

LOUISE; OR, LIFE AND ITS REVEALINGS.

THE MOTHER'S TRIALS, by Charles Burdett.

ALICE GORDON, by Joseph Alden, D. D.

ELLEN HERBERT; OR, FAMILY CHANGES.

MASON'S SELECT REMAINS.

THE LAWYER'S DAUGHTER, by J. Alden, D. D.

AGNES MORRIS; OR, THE HEROINE OF DO-
MESTIC LIFE.

FAMILY PRIDE; OR, THE PALACE AND THE
POOR HOUSE, by Arthur.

THE MORNING OF LIFE; OR, THOUGHTS FOR
THE YOUNG CHRISTIAN, IN PROSE AND
VERSE.

MISCELLANEOUS WORKS,

At One Shilling Each.   *(Cloth Gilt.)*

FLOWERS OF POETRY, Original and Select.

WATTS ON THE IMPROVEMENT OF THE MIND.

FLEETWOOD'S LIFE OF CHRIST.

CPSIA information can be obtained
at www.ICGtesting.com
Printed in the USA
BVOW07s2313280118
506578BV00004B/28/P